Practical
Pre-School

What does it mean to be five?

A practical guide to child development
in the Early Years Early Years Foundation Stage

Jennie Lindon

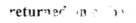

returned on

Contents

Published by Step Forward Publishing Limited
St Jude's Church, Dulwich Road, Herne Hill, London, SE24 0PB Tel. 020 7738 5454
Revised edition © Step Forward Publishing Limited 2008
First edition © Step Forward Publishing Limited 2006
www.practicalpreschool.com

What does it mean to be five? (Revised edition) ISBN: 978 1 904575 42 9

Focus on five-year-olds

What Does it Mean to be Five? explores the developmental needs and likely skills of five-year-olds. This book is complete in itself but five year olds have developed so far along their own personal timeline that the content links closely with the other three titles in this series, especially *What does it mean to be four?* The content of this book is relevant to any practitioner, working with fives anywhere in the UK. The structure of the book, however, follows the framework for England of the Early Years Foundation Stage: guidance covering from birth to five years of age that will be statutory for early years provision from September 2008.

Each book in the *What does it mean to be...?* series recognises that many young children attend some kind of group provision. However, the majority of five-year-olds will now be attending some kind of provision within school grounds. The exception will be where parents have already decided to educate their children at home. This option is a legal possibility, since education is compulsory but school is not. The other possibility is that young children have such profound disabilities and/or complex health conditions that mainstream reception class or primary school is not a realistic option.

So, a considerable proportion of five-year-olds attend reception class or an early year of the primary school system. A proportion of children will consequently also attend some kind of out-of-school provision: breakfast club, after-school and holiday club. Some fives continue with their childminder, who provides the out-of-school support. The objective in this book is to remain consistent with the other titles and approach five-year-olds through their development: as individuals whose uniqueness should not be limited to a role of young 'school pupil'. Children's learning can only be effectively and appropriately supported when adults - practitioners and parents alike - are guided by sound knowledge of child development: what children are like at different ages and what they therefore need in order to thrive.

The layout of each of the four books in this linked series includes:

- Descriptive developmental information within the main text, organised within the six areas of learning used by the Early Years Foundation Stage (England).
- 'For example' sections giving instances of real children and real places and sometimes references to useful sources of further examples.
- 'Being a helpful adult' boxes which focus on adult behaviour that is an effective support for children's learning, as well as approaches that are unfriendly towards young learning.
- 'Food for thought' headings which highlight points of good practice in ways that can encourage reflection and discussion among practitioners, as well as sharing in partnership with parents.

Where are the fives 'officially'?

A different national framework operates in each country of the UK.

- In England from September 2008 the three to five Foundation Stage early years curriculum, will be replaced by the birth to five years framework of the Early Years

Foundation Stage. This framework, just like the Foundation Stage, applies until the end of the reception class, provision that is located within a primary school. Some fives will spend most of the year that they are five within the EYFS, but some will make the move into Year 1 as five-year-olds.

- In Scotland, the Curriculum Framework for Children 3-5 applies to the experiences of fives, but again some five-year-olds have moved into the primary school system. Current developments focus on a Curriculum for Excellence to cover from three to eighteen years of age. In the earlier years, the main focus for development is for a continuity of more active learning and play from the early education of three- to five-year-olds into the initial years of primary school.
- In Wales, many five–year-olds will also be in primary school and experiencing the Foundation Phase curriculum that will apply until they reach seven years. This development aims to take the play-based approach of the early years curriculum into the first years of primary school.
- In Northern Ireland, young children start primary school in the September of the school year after their fourth birthday – so fives will officially be school pupils. The main focus for current development is a Foundation Stage for the first two years of primary school (four- and five-year-olds) that will postpone over-structured educational approaches.

Development matters in the Early Years Foundation Stage (EYFS)

From September 2008 in England many fives will remain 'officially' within a framework that spans the full range of early childhood. All early years practitioners in England need to become familiar with the details of the EYFS, but the good practice described is not new. Part of your task in finding your way around the EYFS materials is recognising just how much is familiar when your provision already has good practice. (See page 70 for information on how to access materials about the EYFS. The EYFS follows the pattern of developmental areas, established with the Foundation Stage, and there are only a few changes within the details of that structure.

There are six areas of learning within the EYFS.

- Personal, Social and Emotional Development
- Communication, Language and Literacy
- Problem Solving, Reasoning and Numeracy
- Knowledge and Understanding of the World
- Physical Development
- Creative Development

This framework is one way of considering the breadth of children's learning. But of course children do not learn in separate compartments; the whole point is that children's learning crosses all the boundaries. The aim of identifying areas of learning is to help adults to create a balance, to address all the different, equally important areas of what children gain across the years of early childhood.

When the EYFS is in place, all these records have to connect with the six areas of learning. A rich resource of developmental information and practice advice is provided in the Practice Guidance booklet of the EYFS, in Appendix 2 that runs from pages 22-114. None of this material should be used as a checklist, or have to-do grids. It is crucial that early years practitioners and teams hold tight to this key point. In each of these very full pages, the same pattern applies.

- The developmental information in the first column, 'Development matters', is a reminder of the kinds of changes likely to happen – not an exhaustive list of what happens, and in this exact way. The examples work like the Stepping Stones guidance of the Foundation Stage.
- The broad and overlapping age spans are deliberate: birth to 11 months, 8-20 months, 16-26 months, 22-36 months, 30-50 months and 40-60+ months. The aim is to refresh about development, supporting practitioners to take time over all the 'steps'. Practitioners, who work with younger children, should not rush to the final early learning goals (ELGs).
- The description of the early learning goals is the only part of all this information that is statutory. The goals only become relevant for observation within the last year of the EYFS (just like with the Foundation Stage), which is the reception class located in primary schools.
- Practitioners working with younger fives will look at the earlier parts of the 40-60+ age band. However, the previous span, of 30-50 months, may be the best starting point if you work with children whose development has been significantly slowed by disability or very limited early experience.
- The ELGs, placed at the end of every 40-60+ age band, are increasingly relevant for observation and assessment of the experience of fives. However, for young fives, wherever they are, there still has to be an awareness of how children are progressing towards those goals. The ELGs are set as expectations for most children to achieve

by the end of the EYFS. The specific point, as defined on page 11 of the statutory guidance is 'by the end of the academic year in which they reach the age of five.'

Child-focussed observation and planning

It will be necessary for practitioners (in England) to adjust their flexible forward planning and child-focussed documentation to reflect the six areas of the EYFS from September 2008. However, the adjustments are minor for those practitioners who have already been working with the Foundation Stage framework. Early years practitioners should have a sound basis of child development knowledge. If any practitioners feel unsure of realistic expectations, then the development matters column should be used as a detailed source of information to build that knowledge across early childhood. Other useful resources, which extend into middle childhood, are given from page 71.

The situation about any kind of written planning and documentation is the same as has applied all the time for the Foundation Stage, namely that there are no statutory written formats for observation and planning. The early years inspection body for England, Ofsted, does not require any specific approach to the need to be observant and to have a planful approach. The EYFS materials offer suggestions, including the flexible approach of the Learning Journey, which is described on the CD ROM materials linked with the 'Principles into Practice card 3.1. Observation, assessment and planning.' But no format is compulsory.

The key messages from the EYFS materials are that any formats used by practitioners need to show:

- The progress of individual children over time, at their own pace and set against realistic expectations for their age, ability and experiences.
- That planning is responsive to the needs and interests of individual children: through continuous provision (the learning environment) and flexible use of planned activities.
- How observations of children make a difference to what is offered to individuals and to sensible short-term changes to planning opportunities for a group of children.
- There is plenty of scope for fine-tuning through short-term planning – that 'what next?' or 'next steps' is a real part of the process.

Over the same pages 22-114 of the EYFS Practice Guidance each page has other information and suggestions:

- 'Look, listen and note' (second column in from the left) is a resource of suggestions, very like the 'Examples of what children do' in the Foundation Stage. This is not a list of the observations everyone has to do; they are reminders of the pitch and level at which it makes sense to observe across that age range.
- The other two columns - 'Effective practice' and 'Planning and resourcing' - are similar to the right hand pages throughout the Foundation Stage file entitled 'What does the practitioner need to do?' Indeed you will find familiar sentences from that resource.

The EYFS also includes the Foundation Stage Profile, with no changes except from 'mathematical development' to 'problem solving, reasoning and numeracy' and changes in wording to a few early learning goals. Known now as the Early Years Foundation Stage Profile, this final record of achievement must be used as the form of assessment over the last year of the EYFS. The profile must be fully completed by the end of June in the academic year in which a child is five years old.

Food for thought

Of course children have started to learn before they encounter experiences offered within the EYFS framework. Young children learn at home with their families, during their time with childminders and in early years settings that offer childcare for children as young as babies.

Good partnership with families must continue to respect what five-year-olds learn with their own parents and that home learning will evolve in a different way from experiences offered in early years provision. Children benefit when practitioners build connections between home and the setting and share accurate information with parents about the EYFS. However, in my professional opinion, parents should never be expected to make family time fit the headings or structure of the early years framework.

For some time now, primary schools in England have given homework to children. I challenge the weight of a curriculum that apparently makes this step necessary. The consequence is that still young children have restrictions on their leisure time – with their own family, their childminder or in their after-school club. A related problem is that the dominance of homework from an early age makes it harder for adults to recognise how non-school time directly contributes to children's learning.

We must not forget that children in reception class are still very young within the span of childhood. Just because they walk through school gates each day does not make them school pupils like six- or seven-year-olds. This aim of this book is to focus on five-years-olds in the context of their overall child development. Since the first edition of this series, I have become even more alert to use of language, including my own.

I have shifted in this edition to talking about early years provision 'on school grounds'. We have to stop saying that five-year-olds (and some four-year-olds) in reception class have 'started school'. I have become very aware that many nursery practitioners talk about their four-year-olds 'leaving us to go to school'. Teams need to talk more accurately about, 'Leaving us to have their final year of the EYFS in reception class'.

Words really do matter, because the consequence is that too many adults – practitioners as well as parents – now refer to children at the end of Year 1 (England) as having experienced 'two years of school'. This statement is sometimes then linked with unrealistic expectations, especially on the literacy front, about what children therefore, 'should have learned by now'.

Judgements against thirteen scales (the same as were established in the Foundation Stage) have to be made from 'assessment of consistent and independent behaviour, predominantly children's self-initiated activities' (page 16 of the statutory guidance).

Young learners

The EYFS guidance stresses how much children need to experience an environment that support the development of a positive disposition to learn. Children are learning about the whole experience of learning as well as gaining knowledge and skills that can be directly observed by practitioners. Early education needs to support or create positive outlooks on learning, in order for children to be well prepared for continuing to learn over their school years. Their EYFS experience needs to enthuse them, helping them to feel competent and able to learn; to realise that they are young learners.

Children in Reception class

Most children will enter provision on school grounds during the EYFS and it has proved a tough task for some reception teams to create or hold onto an appropriate early years curriculum. Pressure has been exerted on some reception staff to get children ready for Key Stage One. Year 1 teachers experience their own pressures and adult anxiety has sometimes rolled down the age bands to nursery teams working with four- and even three-year-olds. The National Literacy Strategy has been especially problematic – and continues to be so - when it has been pushed with limited understanding of how children build up their understanding of early literacy.

As with the four-year-olds, it is so important that reception and year 1 teams are themselves supported and enabled to start with the children themselves. There are high risks in working within a framework for five-year-olds that insists they are now 'pupils'. Young children are then pushed to fit a set of expectations for their behaviour that, placed more responsibly within a child development framework, might never have been viewed as realistic at the outset. I appreciate there is considerable pressure on staff within the school system and some teams still undervalue colleagues who work with the youngest children. However, the function of Foundation Stage never was simply to get children ready for Key Stage One. The early years curriculum guidance valued the time before formal school as important in its own right and the same stance underpins the EYFS.

Children's current learning and potential enthusiasm can be lost in the continued focus to prepare them for the next stage. An accurate, and child-friendly, approach to early childhood has also been undermined by the willingness, even enthusiasm, of many early years practitioners to have their provision described as 'pre-school'. This wording almost inevitably pre-judges early years experiences against preparing children for what the school system wants. The school system should prepare itself for what five- and six-year-olds are genuinely able to manage.

What makes a helpful adult?

The Effective Provision of Pre-School Education (EPPE) project identified key themes from settings with best practice.

- Good learning outcomes for children are linked to adult-child interactions that involve 'sustained shared thinking' and open-ended questioning to extend children's thinking (more on page 35.)
- Practitioners need a thorough knowledge of the curriculum but grounded in sound knowledge and understanding of child development.

- Educational aims need to be shared with parents, but with a respect for how much children learn at home.
- Children benefit from constructive feedback from adults during activities – comments that highlight what has gone well and friendly suggestions for improvement.
- Teams need to establish a positive approach to behaviour, through behaviour policy and practice that encourages problem solving.

the team's judgement, the most effective settings provided a balance which favoured child-itiated over adult-initiated activities. The team described 'child-initiated' events as play activities eely chosen by the children, but from a learning environment and materials that had potential r learning. In many reception classes the balance tipped more and more towards adult-initiated tivities, many in small groups, which gave less scope for patterns of sustained shared thinking.

he pattern seems to be that demands on reception teams mean that practice often becomes eadily more formal and structured. Some reception teams are strong in their practice and ere are a few combined nursery-reception classes or units around the country. But, pressure on ractitioners to move away from a play-based and child-led curriculum seems to be widespread. he EPPE team observed that it is important that Reception and Year 1 teams are supported and iabled to start with the children themselves.

here is considerable pressure on staff within the school system. Experienced ractitioners who support young children have long been regarded as of wer professional status than teachers of older children. Reception and Year teams in many primary schools are under pressure to push on the five-year-lds. In England the pressure of the SATs for seven-year-olds has increased ie perspective that the role of the EYFS is to prepare children for Key Stage Such an outlook - not shared by everyone - creates the risk that younger iildren are mainly seen through the lense of 'pre-': pre-school, pre-Year 1, re-Key Stage 1. Children's current learning and enthusiasms can be lost in ie continued focus to prepare them for the next stage.

What makes a helpful adult?

he Effective Provision of Pre-School Education (EPPE) project identified ey themes from settings with best practice.

- Good learning outcomes for children are linked to adult-child interactions that involve 'sustained shared thinking' and open-ended questioning to extend children's thinking.
- Practitioners need a thorough knowledge of the curriculum, but grounded and sound knwoledge and understanding of child development.
- Educational aims need to be shared with parents, but with a respect for how much children learn at home.
- Children benefit from constructive feedback from adults during activities - comments that highlight what has gone well and friendly suggestions for improvement.
- Teams need to establish a positive approach to behaviour, through behaviour policy and practice that encourages problem solving.

The EPPE team observed that sustained shared thinking for five-year-olds, like their younger versions, was more likely to happen when they were interacting on a one-to-one basis with an adult or with one of their peers. Freely chosen play activities often provided the best opportunitie for adults to extend children's thinking. Five-year-olds are still very young and are not yet developmentally ready to do most of their learning in groups.

The group experience, even in small groups, is hit or miss for five-year-olds and five-year-olds are often in large groups. In the larger groups there is less opportunity for interactive communication. There is also a greater likelihood that the content of a group session will fail to engage five-year-olds or connect with what they already know. Adults working with a large group can easily overlook the sources of confusion for some children.

Five-year-olds, like three- and four-year-olds, need informative and helpful feedback close in time to what they have done or not managed to do, and given in the form of personal interaction. Such feedback is most effectively given in one-to-one interactions or, at most, personal comments in a small group. Large group activities reduce this personal feedback and five-year-olds can remain confused. The risk is even greater when practitioners feel a sense of pressure to continue regardless, because completing a plan for the session is the highest priority (see page 29).

Supporting a positive disposition to learn

The importance of children's attitudes is highlighted in the EYFS document for England. It is made clear that children are not only learning identifiable skills and knowledge, as exciting as that development can be for children and adults alike. The Foundation Stage guidance established that children are learning about the process of learning and about themselves as learners. The guidance states that, 'a positive disposition to learn grows from experiences that children enjoy and can control, are interesting and aid success. Such experiences foster feelings of competence and self-confidence. They motivate children to learn and carry on learning.' The EYFS shares this emphasis.(page 29)

Five-year-olds and rising sixes are beginning to realise that they have a great deal to learn in the future. Some have already encountered frustrating or distressing experiences, where it has become clear to them that they do not understand and perhaps feel left behind in comparison with their peers. Five-year-olds need a positive outlook on themselves as learners if they are not to feel overwhelmed. They need supportive adults - practitioners and parents who work in partnership for the children's well-being.

Young learners

Five-year-olds are moving towards a more uniform educational experience in the form of the National Curriculum. But any discussion of their learning still has to acknowledge the individuality of children.

- Five-year-olds learn by making connections to what they already know or half understand. If five-year-olds are required to make too big a stretch intellectually, the will fall into the 'gap'.
- Healthy emotional development for young children is supported by a growing belief that they are competent individuals. They need a sense of 'I can' and that 'I can't yet' is not a disaster, because adults are there to help children who are struggling or have made a mistake.

- Five-year-olds need to feel supported by adults so that they have the motivation to keep trying, even if something is neither easy nor obvious at the outset.
- They need the constructive feedback that helps them realise that they have managed a new skill or idea. They also need time to enjoy that competence, rather than being rushed on fast to the next intellectual hurdle.
- Enthusiastic and supportive adults help children to develop this positive outlook over the weeks and months. Alternatively, children may learn from negative experiences that they are incompetent, that adults think they keep making mistakes and that there is no point in trying, because you are either 'good at something' or 'useless'.

Being a helpful adult

Practitioners in Reception classes work with ratios that require them to share themselves out between the children, often in what feels like a very thin spread. Adults have to make the most of the opportunities, bearing in mind how much children need constructive feedback that helps them focus on what has gone well, not just what has gone wrong.

- Young children need to see themselves as learners now, and that they have learned already. Your familiarity with individual children can enable you, along with their parents, to remind the children of specific examples of what they have learned in the past. Such support can help them especially when they are struggling at the moment.
- You can support children to feel that 'useful mistakes' and 'handy wrong turns' are not disasters but can be helpful, because adults can spot what is confusing or only partly understood by the children. Your behaviour, words and body language will give the message to children that it is fine to ask for help.
- In a busy Reception group, it can be a useful strategy to coach children in the difference between wanting something said again and needing something phrased differently. Helpful adults can explain, and demonstrate, that sometimes we need to say, 'I didn't hear' or 'can you say that again, please?' But this request is different from 'I'm confused' or 'I don't understand', because this request means 'please say it in a different way'.
- Of course, adults then need to follow this clue that whatever was said before needs to be rephrased, perhaps shown as well as told, and not simply repeated.
- You may need to break down a skill or idea into smaller steps. Go back with a child or small group to the point at which they are competent or can understand. Then work on with them from that point of confidence, in order to tackle what is confusing, difficult or even, perhaps, too hard for now.
- Useful and courteous phrases can be, 'you don't understand this at the moment' or 'you can't do this yet....' Children can then

hear in your voice the sense that things can change; not knowing or struggling need not go on and on.

- Acknowledgement and an offer of help can be made with, 'I can see that you're finding this tough. Shall we see how I can help?' or 'that was a handy mistake you made, because now I understand where you get stuck. Can I show you....?'
- Be generous with time to appreciate, acknowledge and admire. Adults need to celebrate successes with children, often with friendly words and the respect of attention by looking and listening with genuine interest.
- Celebration does not always have to be lengthy or involve symbols like stickers. Five-year-olds accept the stickers and certificates that are part of the incentive systems established in many reception classes, and which reflect the pattern of the primary school. However, it is unwise to create the expectation for young children that external reward – although of the symbolic nature of stickers – is more important than personal satisfaction.

Practitioners working with young children in the final year of the EYFS will focus increasingly on the early learning goals. This book now discusses development within each of the six areas of learning defined by the EYFS, and the early learning goals are provided within the appropriate section. Each goal benefits from a reflective adult approach along the lines of:

- In what ways will this goal be realistic for children at the end of the EYFS, especially since some will still be young fives?
- What kind of learning or disposition is described in this goal and what will it look like when shown by five-year-olds: what will you observe?
- In order to achieve this goal, and interpret it realistically, what will children need from supportive adults?

- What could be an unrealistic interpretation of this goal – one that fails to fit realistic expectations based on knowledge of child development?
- How can supportive adults bring this goal alive? In what ways do you, can you, set a good example in this instance? Can you show this learning or pattern of behaviour through your own actions and words day by day?

Personal, Social and Emotional Development

Five-year-olds can be intrigued, keen to find out and to share their skills and knowledge. In a supportive environment they are able to direct and pursue their own interests, as well as ask for and appreciate input from adults. A dilemma, even a problem, for some five-year-olds can be that their enthusiasm and self-direction may not be welcomed in increasingly more formal educational settings. Helpful early years practitioners do not use sight of the fact that PSED remains just as important for five-year-olds as for young children.

Good professional practice within any Reception class will be genuinely child-friendly and developmentally appropriate for five-year-olds (and for the fours who are in many Reception classes). I stress the problems that can develop for children when the final year of their early childhood provision becomes too school-like. So it is equally important to emphasise that I have been privileged to observe some excellent practice in Reception classes. A major strand of good practice - and often of rethinking the Reception experience - is a willingness to address PSED. These school teams accept that children need to feel emotionally safe and personally valued, and not only in Reception. The other major factor is a focus on child-initiated learning, and adult enthusiasm for what excites children today. Observation, flexible forward planning and recording is highly influenced by how children play, what they want to say and how their interests have been engaged.

Early Years Foundation Stage strand - Dispositions and attitudes
- Continue to be interested, excited and motivated to learn
- Be confident to try new activities, initiate ideas and speak in a familiar group
- Maintain attention, concentrate and sit quietly when appropriate

Competent five-year-olds

Five-year-olds vary in confidence but many can make choices and express their ideas and opinions. Five-year-olds can speak up in a familiar group but because the dynamics of groups vary, as does the behaviour of the adult leading the group, they will sometimes decide that an adult does not really listen or is impatient, and so contributing is not a pleasant experience. Even in well run groups, many five-year-olds find it hard to hang onto an exciting thought. There is still a short gap between their thinking something interesting and wanting to share it out loud.

Five-year-olds can be attentive, using their skills of looking and listening. They are often able to keep one thought ticking over while they attend to something else in terms of action or listening to the words of others. Five-year-olds have also usually grasped the important understanding in group life, that adults sometimes give an instruction or item of information to the whole group. Just because an adult does not say your name, it does not necessarily mean that the message is not for you, too. However, there are definite limits to how long five-year-olds can concentrate, specially if they are required to stay still, possibly in an uncomfortable seating position. Supportive practitioners in Reception classes or out-of-school settings need to be realistic about how long they expect children to concentrate while sitting still. The words 'when appropriate' in this goal need careful thought. (See also the comments about physical alertness and mental liveliness on page 54.)

Life within a Reception (or Year 1) class requires five-year-olds to be reasonably motivated, self-directed and to understand the rhythms of daily routines and sequences. Even in the best organised and caring classroom, young children have to manage with an adult-child ratio that provides limited, personal adult attention. Adults owe it to children to understand what it feels like as a five-year-old to cope with the demands of a school day.

- What is required? In what ways is the day different from what children have known before?
- To what extent does early years provision within school grounds demand that all children fit the role of 'pupil'? Or does the whole team working on this school site acknowledge and respect the perspective of the youngest children?
- What do five- and six-year-olds find confusing or daunting? Are adults aware and do they adjust?

The realities of transition into primary school life and routines are also discussed from page 22.

Early Years Foundation Stage strand- Self-confidence and self-esteem

- Respond to significant experiences, showing a range of feelings when appropriate
- Have a developing awareness of their own needs, views and feelings and be sensitive to the needs, views and feelings of others
- Have a developing respect for their own cultures and beliefs and those of other people

---

Five-year-olds and emotional development

Five-year-olds can have developed noticeably in emotional literacy: their ability to recognise and express their own feelings and an awareness of the feelings of others. These Early Learning Goals need to be considered in a reflective way by supportive adults, with a full recognition that social learning within children's development is not only about the five-year-olds; adult behaviour is crucial.

- The questions need to be asked: 'who decides what are "significant experiences"?' and 'when are feelings "appropriate" or not?'
- Expectations need to be realistic, for instance some five-year-olds are caring but no child should be expected to be sensitive all the time. Most adults would fail such a tough requirement.
- The last two goals in the set (see above) need to be viewed in connection with the goals in the 'sense of community' strand (see page 24). Five-year-olds can show empathy and altruism in their dealings with their peers and adults, but they have the right to expect respect, care and consideration in return from

Food for thought

Positive experiences in circle time or other forms of supported group discussion can build five- and six-year-old skills towards effective group participation. The basis is built for the articulate give-and-take that takes place in those primary schools that carry out proper consultation with children and in the group discussion meetings that are run in some out-of-school care settings.

The advantage of out-of-school care can be the opportunities for supported mixed-age discussions within club meetings. However, some primary schools also create such opportunities through school councils. The adults have a responsibility to ease discussion, but older children are often sensitive to bringing in younger or less confident children. Of course, adults can do a lot to help to create a positive environment, but they do not then have to do all the work. (See also page 21 for a further discussion of what makes circle time work for children.)

adults, as well as other children. Indeed, a crucial part of these goals is the adult contribution of setting a good example through their own behaviour.

All the points in *What Does it Mean to be Three?* and *What Does it Mean to be Four?* about support for children's emotional development are equally relevant for five-year-olds. Five-year-olds can show empathy and a grasp of subtle social situations. However, their learning is poorly supported, and can actually be undermined if adults are insensitive, either in informal conversation or in the circle time that is now part of many nurseries and primary school days (see page 28). For children to develop towards these goals, they need plenty of experiences that show them that other people, children and adults, are genuinely sensitive to and interested in them as individuals. General topics about 'our feelings' or very general circle time discussion will not work in isolation. It is also inappropriate to encourage children to speak out about very personal issues in what is actually a public forum. Children need to develop a relationship of trust with a practitioner, such that they feel able to talk in confidence. Time and adult attention are at a premium in many Reception classes. But sensitive adults can make the most of conversations that arise, that enable children to receive personal attention for what interests or concerns them.

Five- and six-year-olds grow in emotional security when they feel confident they have someone to turn to who will take their concerns seriously. Five-year-olds need to know that their emotions are recognised. Children feel they are taken seriously when adults reply with comments like, 'I understand that you really don't like all the noise in the lunch hall' rather than, 'there's nothing to be upset about' or even, 'don't be silly'.

Articulate children of primary school age are able to explain, and complain, that teachers, playground assistants and parents often do not listen properly. Children need to feel that the playground problems they voice are taken seriously. They do not appreciate empty clichés like, 'ignore them and they'll stop' or 'don't play with them then'. Such phrases only demonstrate that adults do not understand or choose not to give their time to grasp why there is no easy answer to problems between friends, social groups or the sharing of space in school grounds.

Five- and six-year-olds develop respect for others through experiencing respect themselves; it is a two-way process. They learn problem-solving skills from adults who listen, discuss possible options and offer support. This approach can help even four- and five-year-olds to make a decision about their current problem. However, young children can also learn more general strategies about how to consider and resolve problems. Some children who are six and seven years of age understand that adults cannot solve everything, especially problems that arise when the adult is not present. But even children this young will sometimes say that talking about a problem helps and can make you feel better enough to face it, even if there is no easy answer.

For example

Five-year-old problem-solving skills and the confidence to speak up can be seen in Reception classes with responsive teams, in family homes and in out-of-school care.

The Balham Family Centre team has aimed to create an atmosphere in which the children feel able to voice their own concerns. The main activities are with mixed ages but their special age-banded afternoon sessions were developed when a delegation of nine- and ten-year-olds proposed that they should have their own club. These older children wanted to solve the perceived problem that younger children got in the way of favourite activities of the nine to elevens. A separate club was not feasible but a problem-solving conversation led to an over-nines afternoon. When the ver-nines session was established, the younger children, including the five- and six-year-olds, felt ble to speak up and say that they, too, would like their own special time when they could plan heir own play programme with their group worker.

Like many after school and holiday clubs, Buck's Kids Club in Leek has a wide age range that can o from four-year-olds up to ten- or eleven-year-olds. The club team have thought about how to se the different rooms in the house, which is their premises, so that the younger age range can pread out with activities that will absorb them. Adults are easily available for all the children, ut the older ones have an outdoor area, covered by a simple canopy and their own room, on he top floor, where they can relax and organise themselves. These older boys and girls feel espected because they are not required to follow the same pattern as younger children. Also they ome to get their snack from the same room as the younger ones but are welcome to take it and at elsewhere with their age peers. (See page 74 for details of people and places mentioned in xamples.)

Social development, friends and friendliness

The importance of touch and friendly physical contact is aised in each book in this series, because he need for friendly communication hrough touch extends throughout early hildhood – and into middle childhood. ives, just like their younger selves, need o feel emotionally safe and at ease with heir important adults in out-of-home provision. Fives are unlikely to need a eassuring cuddle as often as younger hildren. They also appreciate, through he evidence of their eyes, that adult attention is now spread more thinly petween all the children. Nevertheless, a five-year-old who is unhappy for some reason or who has been physically hurt n a fall, will feel personally rejected if here is no prospect of reassurance and comfort from touch.

However, just like with younger children, fives still want to be able to say 'hello, I'm back!' with a full body hug, when hey have been absent for some reason. A warm relationship matters, so they may also want to show by touch, as well as say in words, to their practitioner, 'I've missed you – are you better now?' Fives want, and deserve, the relaxed emotional atmosphere that leaves everyone at ease with touch and hugs that say 'haven't we done brilliantly!' I have been in infant schools where children think their cook is a wonderful person (who also produces lovely food – very important for healthy habits). In one school, the cook's appearance from the kitchen to walk towards the dining hall, provoked a rush of children to hug 'hello' and ask 'what have you got for our lunch today?'

An emotionally healthy atmosphere – for early years provision and primary schools - is one where these scenes will be regarded as positive and without problems. Unfortunately for children's development, this is not the case in many settings. Restrictions on communication through physical contact have become entangled in some settings with a serious misunderstanding about good safeguarding practice. Practitioners have been made anxious about the risk of allegations of sexual abuse and sometimes about negative consequences of using adult strength wisely to keep children safe from hurting themselves and others. This problem of 'adult protection' seems to be especially fraught in some schools and so affects provision, not only within reception class, located on school grounds.

Readers who face this practice dilemma will need to seek further advice around genuinely protective practice with children. I explore the concerns and the best practice decisions in detail in my *Safeguarding children and young people* (see page 72). The main point is that all practitioners must focus on the 'child' in 'child protection'. There are no national requirements – arising from child protection guidance or any other framework - that demand practitioners follow no-touch regimes, that will undermine children's personal and social development. Nor is there any support for an adult reluctance to meet five-year-olds' continuing need for occasional help in their personal care, for instance over toileting accidents. Schools, that impose a policy that parents must be called under these circumstances, are not supported by national guidance. They are open to legitimate criticism for creating avoidable embarrassment and distress for the children. They can also be challenged on equality grounds when children additionally have a disability that means such events are inevitable.

Five-year-olds need the choice to make their own friends and some friendships based on shared interests and activities will cross gender, social class and cultural boundaries. Although boys and girls may still sometimes play together, the gender lines tend to be drawn more firmly now. Good practice has an equality practice dimension, but practitioners have to be attuned to the five-year-old social world.

- Children want adults to support them when they are on the receiving end of offensive words or unkind behaviour. If they experience, and observe support, then they are far more likely to adjust their behaviour in response to firm guidance.
- Five-year-olds, and the older children in school, are deeply unimpressed by what has been called the 'hierarchy of hurt' approach, that some forms of offensiveness are more reprehensible than others.
- Adults may feel it is fair and makes sense in terms of adult social inequality to target especially offensiveness on the basis of race, gender or disability. But this selectivity is not perceived as fair by the children. Children of primary school age can be deeply hurt by personally offensive remarks about, for instance, being adopted, having eczema or nasty remarks about their mum.
- Simplistic adult interpretations of equality practice sometimes allow only for one direction of unpleasantness. Some adults assume that sexist remarks can only be from boys to girls. Or they may assume that threats to positive identity are only an issue for children from what are seen as minority ethnic groups.
- All practitioners are responsible for addressing inequalities that can be observed within the setting and any issues that affect social inclusion. Such factors can affect children from a wide range of social and cultural groups. Children from

ethnic minority groups may experience discriminatory attitudes in the local neighbourhood, which are imported into school by other children. However, 'white' children from very deprived backgrounds can have a fragile group cultural identity. In the absence of specific support, they may build a positive sense of self by derogatory attitudes to ethnic groups they classify as different to themselves.

Early Years Foundation Stage strands -

Making relationships
- Form good relationships with adults and peers
- Work as part of a group or class, taking turns and sharing fairly, understanding that there need to be agreed values and codes of behaviour for groups of people, including adults and children, to work together harmoniously

Behaviour and self-control

- Understand what is right, what is wrong and why
- Consider the consequences of their words and actions for themselves and others

Social skills and group life

Happy social contact and friendships are important to children. Projects in which young children are asked for their views about nursery or school usually find that children spontaneously focus on the importance of friends. A positive attraction of early years settings and happy playgrounds is the opportunity to play and chat with friends. Children in primary school describe the school playground as a lonely place when you have no friends and you cannot manage to join any existing groups. Five-year-olds can have made close friendships already and these can last when children move on together from nursery or pre-school into the same Reception class. Five-year-olds have their quarrels and off days, but some childhood friendships last from nursery into the adult years.

Many of the social skills discussed in *What Does it Mean to be Three?* (see page 16) are still utterly relevant for five-year-olds and rising sixes. If adults are honest, we continue to face grown-up versions of these social choices, dilemmas and situations that are genuinely hard to resolve. Five-year-olds are able often to form 'good relationships' but that does not mean that relationships with adults, friendships with peers and temporary alliances always run smoothly.

- With experience, many five-year-olds have strategies for how to approach an existing group of children and to join the activity without usually being rejected. Such strategies do not always work and some groups may effectively be closed to new children.
- However, many five-year-olds are welcoming of children who approach with consideration and even these young children can be caring of children who are new arrivals to their class or to the neighbourhood.

- Children often find difficulties in coping with children who want to spend more time with them than they would like. Children sometimes also want to be on their own for a while.

Once five-year-olds have joined the life of a primary school their social skills are of high relevance in play and playground interactions. Break time matters a great deal to children and practitioners need to recognise that this time is as much a part of the school day to five-year-olds and older children as classroom time (see also page 58). Children have to bring their social skills to bear on choice, organisation, time management and conflict situations within the school grounds and they want adult support at such times. Wise infant or primary teams work from reception class onwards to value the importance for children of their play. Increasingly play in school means breaktime out on the playground.

For example

In my visits to Crabtree Infants School it was a pleasure to see in action how the entire school team, led by the head, placed a significant importance on the outdoor areas of the school and on children's time outside.

- The reception class had their own outdoor space and were given time to get used to the larger area available to the slightly older children. This well- resourced space became familiar to five-year-olds through visits and they could see the enjoyment they would have when they joined Year 1.
- The entire team valued children's time outdoors and one practitioner had been enabled to take particular responsibility to develop and equip the outdoor spaces. Children, who had left reception, had not lost their opportunity to play outdoors. Their outdoor space was well equipped with play resources and space to spread out in lively physical games. Adults were ready to join in any way that supported children's play choices today.

Problems can arise because children form groups and isolated children try to join in ongoing games and are rejected. Five-year-olds and older children may need sensitive support from playground staff, when they find it hard to enter play, and not simply demands to the existing group that they 'let her play with you'. Adults also need to be observant and not leap to conclusions. Some children are not allowed to join in because they have repeatedly broken the rules and 'spoiled' the play. Adults in the playground need to set a good example in asking, 'what has happened?' rather than assuming that the existing group has been unkind. Sometimes the other children have tolerated the rejected child and explained the rules of play more than once, until their patience was exhausted.

The work of consultants like Wendy Titman has highlighted that responsive school teams are needed to support children's learning in the outdoor area just as much as inside the Reception or Year 1 classroom. Key issues include:

- Listening to the children who have a clear idea of the process and problems in playground life.
- Adults need to set a good example in problem-solving rather than imposing solutions or punitive actions in which children are uninvolved and often judged to be 'so unfair!'
- A whole-school team approach is essential, otherwise children, even the youngest, sense that non-teaching support staff in the playground are of lower status than teachers and do not deserve respect.

- Likewise, a whole-school positive behaviour policy needs to be integrated with playground life and the actions of playground staff.

The importance of having friends at break time in school grounds is recognised by the organisation Learning Through Landscapes (more information on page 72). They have developed the idea of the friendship stop and the friendship squad. The aim of this practical idea is that an agreed welcoming location is established in a school playground. The focus may be a natural feature like a tree or an area with seating rather like a bus stop. Children who find themselves without play companions can stop at the agreed location. The named members (children) on friendship squad duty today are responsible for noticing any child. They then go across and keep the child company, sometimes just chatting.

The ability of children to support their peers is an untapped resource in many schools. The practical ideas of the friendship squad require some adult support, but then the children undertake the befriending. Hilary Stacey and Pat Robinson describe how children can be taught the skills of mediation to apply in the playground. Conflict resolution skills can be taught to children as young as four years of age and, so long as the school team is committed, can become part of the Personal, Social and Health Education (PSHE) element of the National Curriculum.

Children as young as nine and ten years old have become effective playground supporters, known in different schools as conflict busters or buddies. These children then use their skills to enable their peers to deal with conflict in a non-aggressive way. These children are in middle childhood but the skills they use can have been steadily learned with adult support from five and six years of age.

For example

Five-year-olds like sometimes to play with younger children but they also benefit from contact with older children. School classrooms work on a narrow age band, although the ages mix in the school playground. In contrast, out-of-school care settings cope with a wide age band of children within the same club or holiday playscheme. The social interactions are a reminder that children play with their age peers but often form alliances, temporary and more long lasting, across the years of childhood.

In my visit to Poplar Play Centre there were some five-, six- and seven-year-olds who attended as part of the holiday playscheme. These were the older children in this setting and they spent some time together but also mixed with younger children (see examples on page 21 or 63). These older children were used to the play centre and sensitive to the ground rules as well as aware of the much younger children. Because the total numbers of children were lower than in term time, the morning started with open movement between the different parts of the garden. Although the gate from the younger children's outdoor area was open, both the younger and older children hesitated at the invisible barrier, checking with an adult that it was all right to cross.

The team of Cool Kids at St Josephs are aware of the age range in the after-school club as well as their holiday playscheme. The team works to help the older ones to be sensitive to what the five-year-olds can manage and their smaller size. The aim is to increase awareness in a friendly way, without nagging.

Given a choice in after-school care, children often want some contact across the age ranges, so long as there are some breaks. KidsComeFirst in Colchester previously divided club activities by age but changed in response to the input of the children, who said they did not want this division. An age split kept siblings apart and this separation was especially felt by the younger sibling. The club has moved to a range of planned activities and play areas that enables five- and six-year-olds to use the home corner or dressing up, but older children also have easy access.

Older children in an out-of-school setting can be competent in organising the younger ones and caring, so long as they are not required to make adjustments all the time. The older children in Cool Kids at St Josephs have chosen in some holiday times to organise tournaments, with teams and a score keeper, and activities like a talent show. The practitioners help as requested and watch out for the younger ones, but there are advantages for older children engaging with the younger ones. Five- and six-year-olds can experience a working example of what the 'big boys and girls' can do.

Moral behaviour and understanding

Five-year-olds have progressed some way in their understanding of moral issues:

- Five-year-olds can have a good grasp of the 'why' and are able to explain in turn, so long as they have had simple explanations that make sense in their social world. They can be more able to appreciate the reciprocal nature of positive behaviour: we listen to each other, I consider your feelings and you consider mine.
- Five-year-olds are now old enough, however, to notice and draw attention to inconsistencies in adult behaviour and at least some five-year-olds will comment, if only within their peer group, about adults (school staff or parents) who 'tell us to …. But they don't!'
- Five-year-olds are also more able to handle speculative, 'what should he/she do..?' scenarios, so long as they are grounded in a situation, perhaps from a story, that the children can envisage. Speculation about moral alternatives has to make sense in terms of meaningful situations for a five-year-old.
- Five-year-olds are often more able to allow for simple alternative motives underlying behaviour, such as 'It was an accident; he didn't mean to tread on my fingers.'

Five-year-olds can have a clear idea of rules within a familiar setting: Reception class, out-of-school care and family home. They are able to follow simple, positively phrased rules that make sense in terms of familiar routines. The ideas of 'right' and 'wrong' can only make sense in a familiar context. So the Early Learning Goal covering that area has to be grounded by responsive adults in terms of what makes sense in a five-year-old social world. Adults must also remain realistic; children, like adults, sometimes know what they should do but, for all kinds of reasons, choose not to do it. Sometimes it is hard to do the right thing.

Five- and six-year-olds are also able, with a supportive adult, to consider a problem area or time for which a ground rule may be helpful. So children of this age can have a grasp of why rules can be useful, so long as adults do not become too abstract in their explanations or requirements. However, five-year-olds have also built up their own expectations and a framework for ground rules and have strong sense of social justice. Fairness is important and five- and six-year-olds can lose respect for adults who are inconsistent, have favourites or who blatantly do not follow their own rules.

For example

The Balham Family Centre in South London has developed ground rules for the Latchkey Project within their overall behaviour management policy. These rules apply from their youngest five-year-olds to their eldest (eleven years old).

The code was drafted in consultation with the children themselves and it is reviewed on a regular basis, to reflect children's views and the way that they wish to express the rules. For instance, part of the 'respect' ground rule is 'no swearing, cussing or name calling', since 'cussing' is the term that the children currently use locally and they know what it means. The children's ground rules include a Street Behaviour Code, discussed because of the practical need to keep children safe as they are walked from their primary schools to the family centre.

Rules such as walking with a partner make sense to the children, even the five-year-olds. There is a practical ground rule that everyone stops talking in order to pay attention as they all cross the road. The practitioners remind the children with courtesy and they obey the rule themselves. The centre has had feedback from parents that their children have explained and wanted to follow the ground rule when they are out with the family.

Once the Latchkey rules were established, the team realised that they needed to work on guidelines for adult behaviour: what the adults needed to do in order to support the children in wanted behaviour. This step is a reminder that children learn far more effectively when the adults recognise their role in the social learning process.

For example

In Poplar Play Centre, several children of different ages were having fun on a four-seater rocker that operated on a large spring.

Two-year Chloe and three-year-old Charlotte got onto the rocker. They were joined by five-year-old Kayleigh and Alric, who was three. Alric soon looked uneasy at the vigorous rocking and the girls stopped to let him get off swiftly. The remaining three children liked the fierce movement and rocking deeply to and fro. Jack (two and a half) got onto the empty fourth seat. There were lots of giggles and fierce rocking. Jack was not too happy and the girls stopped for him to get off. Jack was then happy to watch from a slight distance and grinned as a happy observer. At one point Chloe had slipped a bit off her seat and Kayleigh steadied the rocker with her foot so that Chloe could sit more squarely.

Isobelle (nearly two) left a two-person rocker nearby to come and watch the girls on the four-seater rocker. She edged steadily closer to the rocker and I moved over to guide her back. Three girls on the rocker were already looking warily at Isobelle and how close she was approaching. They looked pleased that I had guided Isobelle back a couple of paces; 'because she's little' they said.

Food for thought

- Many primary schools consider how to manage the transition and entry for children and their parents. Some offer a considerate programme of induction to parents and children alike.
- Partnership with parents is, of course, good practice because parents will be central to supporting their child through the changes. It is respectful of schools to recognise that the parent-child relationship is already of long standing. The familiar phrase used by school teams of 'new parents' is not really courteous. Mothers and fathers are not new to parenting; they are developing a new relationship with the school, becoming 'school parents'. The phrase 'new parents' makes no more sense than to call the staff 'new teachers'.
- But it is equally important to see this transition from the five-year-olds' perspective. There is often much discussion about preparing children for school. It is only the more reflective and sensitive school teams that think about preparing school for children and learning about those parts of the building or routines that five-year-olds find most disconcerting.

This example, like others I observed during my visit to Poplar Play, was a reminder that children of diverse ages play happily together. Kayleigh, as the eldest and with the longest legs, took a careful role on occasion to steady the rocker but all the girls were equal participants.

How five-year-olds handle times of conflict, minor or major, depends a great deal on their experience so far. They can have learned the motivation and skills to use listening and talking through when faced with a conflict, but five-year-olds who opt for talking, rather than shouting or hitting, have gained this skill and preference from experience and adults who have set a good example (see learning the skills of conflict resolution in *What Does it Mean to be Four?* page 17)

Undoubtedly, there can be uncomfortable dilemmas for some children when they move between settings. Five-year-olds can have learned skills of talking through and of an assertive approach to disagreements, but then they meet practitioners in a different setting, or even a different part of the same school setting. Some of these adults may not value, nor possibly understand, five-year-olds' skills of negotiation and assertiveness. Children may find themselves labelled as 'cheeky' or 'rude', simply because they express an opinion different from that of the adult.

Five-year-olds are able to cope to an extent with different expectations in different settings within their social world, usually between different parts of an extended family or between home and out-of-home provision. However, very significant differences between home and early years provision, or school life, can be extremely difficult for five-year-olds to handle, because the different rules and underlying philosophy point to different behaviour. For example, a child whose family say firmly, 'hit back, don't be a wimp!', in contrast to practitioners who say, 'we don't hit people here'. The potential conflict can be even harder to handle if the message from home is of disrespect for early years practitioners or the school staff.

Early Years Foundation Stage strand - Self-care

- Dress and undress independently and manage their own personal hygiene
- Select and use activities and resources independently

A nurturing environment supports growing independence

The EYFS focuses on the importance of the learning environment for children – indoors and outdoors. But the guidance also valuably distinguishes the emotional environment – most clearly in the Principles into Practice card 3.3. about 'The Learning Environment'. This guidance is a timely reminder that the practical implications of PSED really matters. A nurturing environment is integral to responsible practice with children - not an optional extra.

Marjorie Boxall, an educational psychologist in London during the 1970s, dealt with many referrals of children whom teachers found hard to manage in the classroom. Her observations led her to develop small nurture groups.

A revival of interest in the 1990s has led to the re-emergence of nurture groups. The high adult-child ratio is more expensive than the usual Reception or Year 1 ratio, but in the long term the expense is much less than the social cost of letting children fail at school. The work highlights

The ways in which disruptive early experiences of different kinds can mean that children have not built any understanding of a predictable social world.

In the nurture groups, children experience the rhythm of caring routines, physical contact and adults who show consistent affection for the children as individuals. They need safe time and space to be the two- and three-year-olds that their previous experiences blocked. The high adult-child ratio and emphasis on caring routine helps to create a sense of security for children who have not developed an idea of a familiar and safely predictable day.

In the nurture groups, children of five, six and older are enabled to experience early years learning activities that they have missed. However, the way in which the group is run is as important as the activities. The children need a regular routine as well as variety in daily events. The objective is to combine a nurturing approach with a supportive daily structure. Children are then enabled to learn social skills crucial to group life, such as taking turns, making choices and seeing an activity through to completion. The children also need to develop a trust in adults and see them as a useful resource.

Five-year-olds can be competent in their skills of self-care, although they are still young and appreciate help sometimes with tricky fastenings and food that is not easy to cut. Self-reliance matters a great deal to five-year-olds, because their skills distinguish them from the 'little ones'. Of course, many five-year-olds are having to negotiate a transition that puts them right back as the little ones' themselves as they enter the Reception class in primary school. Time constraints and routines may put pressure on five-year-olds' skills of self-care:

- Competent dressers can nevertheless struggle when they experience tight time limits for getting dressed and undressed for physical activities indoors or outside. It is important that adults continue to help and show friendly support for children who struggle with shoes or fastenings.
- Competent eaters can feel troubled by the noise and crowds of a packed lunchtime hall or canteen. New skills are needed, such as negotiating lots of people, finding a table, eating a cooked or packed lunch within a short space of time and handling new tidying-up arrangements. Supportive Reception teams often plan a steady introduction for children to the main school lunch location.
- As well as food, children need easy access to water. Being thirsty, or even dehydrated in hot weather, makes children unhappy and unable to concentrate. Schools vary considerably in how much they make drinking water available.

Unless children have disabilities that affect this skill, five-year-olds will be able to manage in the toilet without help. But going to the toilet in primary school is different from nursery or a separate Reception unit. Five-year-olds increasingly have to hold on and anticipate that they need to go to the toilet, rather than simply go to the toilets within their familiar territory. Children also need to be told that the 'big' children go to separate boys' and girls' toilets.

Reception teams who have listened to the children often find that they seriously dislike the school toilets. Reasonable complaints tend to include that some toilets are dark and scary, that they smell, that essential products like toilet paper and soap run out and that there is no privacy (either because no locks are permitted or because other children barge in). Supportive Reception and Year 1 staff have championed the five- and six-year-olds to make a difference in those aspects that most distress the children.

For example

The school team at Welholme Infants School, led by their head, focus on children's personal, social and emotional development as the crucial underpinning of five- and six-year-olds' experience of their primary school.

There is a strong focus on understanding what range of experiences the children bring as they start the transition to being a pupil. What are the children, or their parents, likely to find more straightforward and what may be difficult? There is an equally strong focus on helping children to feel like learners and using the school curriculum to support the positive disposition to learn. So, planning for the days of children in Reception is strong on creative activities. This part of the curriculum is the means to support other skills that the children need to learn, but at a pace that is possible for them.

Early Years Foundation Stage strand - Sense of community
- Understand that people have different needs, views, cultures and beliefs, which need to be treated with respect
- Understand that they can expect others to treat their needs, views, cultures and beliefs with respect

The school as a community for children

When they are asked, five-year-olds can explain what they find difficult, or less enjoyable, as they experience the approach of reception class – especially if it is very different from nursery routine. Observant adults can also tune into children's concerns and sensitive reception teams take their time in easing children into the more difficult aspects of life on school grounds. I have built the following list

- Reception teams, who have listened to the children, realise that five-year-olds can initially feel overwhelmed by the size of the spaces they have to negotiate. Corridors may seem long and stairs endless. A school that eventually feels familiar is a confusing and large place at the outset.
- Five-year-olds can be confused about where they are allowed to go. They need to be helped to understand how everyone moves around the building: walking rather than running. But when all the children are on the move, the corridors and stairs can feel crowded, even risky, when you are the smallest of the school population.
- Reception and Year 1 teams need to work to ease children's transition from the greater flexibility of nursery and Reception to greater structure in Year 1. Reception and Year 1 classrooms can be different, yet sensitive teams work hard to avoid a sudden change for the children.
- It is inevitable that five- and six-year-olds will realise that the school curriculum moves towards less choice and access to materials than in nursery. Children recognise the greater constraints of time, less opportunities often for relaxed conversation, more time in groups and more structured routines. Yet Reception and Year 1 staff can be supportive in using such flexibility as exists and recognising the value of playtime, when children enjoy chatting with attentive adults as well as their friends.
- Full school assembly can be a daunting prospect for five- and six-year-olds. The hall is probably large and full of children, seating may feel cramped and the end result can

feel noisy and crowded. Again, wise Reception, and even Year 1, teams insist that the children do not have to have to join full assembly straightaway. Smaller gatherings and short visits can help, as can talking children through what will happen in a school assembly.

Five- and six-year-olds most likely have enough sense of themselves as individuals that they now have some understanding of themselves as members of groups: their own family, their neighbourhood and the school as a community of significance for them. How children are treated in Reception and the broader school community will shape their ability to be sensitive in their turn.

In her consultations with school teams and children, Wendy Titman showed how the school grounds, and any changes that adults made, gave clear messages to the children about their place in this community. In *Special Places, Special People* Wendy Titman explained how, '…school grounds give out coded messages to the children who use them about their identity as part of a group of "users". Are they expected to be "carers", "big tough sports players", "hiders and seekers", "horticulturalists", "confident occupiers of space", "involved with the elements", " a young animal", a "socialised proto-adult" or what?' (page 16). Children drew their own conclusions from the level of care given by adults to the school grounds and rules about access to playground areas. Wendy Titman noted, where children believed that the grass could not be used because it would get damaged, they read this as meaning that the grass was more important to the school than they were, particularly where playtime on tarmac was unpleasant, uncomfortable, boring and in their view dangerous.' (page 35) When the school grounds were poorly maintained, with rubbish or damaged items, the children expressed the view that people did not care about them, the children.

You will find more about school grounds under 'Physical Development' on page 58 and about children's awareness of the broader community under 'Knowledge and Understanding of the World' on page 51. There is further discussion about consultation with children under 'Communication, Language and Literacy' on page 29.

Communication, Language and Literacy

Five-year-olds and rising sixes can be articulate and skilful communicators. Given appropriate early experiences, fives also have skills of listening to others – peers and adults. They have begun to make sense of the world of written language and have some understanding of what is yet to come for their learning. Confident fives use their communication skills and emerging literacy beyond their hours in reception class. However, it is crucial for young learners that adult expectations are properly grounded in knowledge of child development.

Early Years Foundation Stage strands

Language for communication
- Sustain attentive listening, responding to what they have heard with relevant comments, questions or actions
- Speak clearly and audibly with confidence and control and show awareness of the listener.

Language for thinking
- Use language to imagine and recreate roles and experiences
- Use talk to organise, sequence and clarify thinking, ideas, feelings and events

Five-year-olds' skills of communication

Five-year-olds and rising sixes can be impressive talkers and listeners. Their spoken communication can be a window onto their thinking and thoughts in progress. The early learning goals focus on this development in the context of children's last year in the EYFS. But five-year-olds do not only use their communication skills within their reception class. It is important to use awareness of children's full experience in order to ground adult expectations. Practitioners can be surprised by conversations that children have at home. But also a shift to more open-ended experiences – especially those that tap into their imagination – sometimes released an unexpected flow of talk.

- Five-year-olds are likely to have a substantial, in some instances an impressive, vocabulary. Children vary, depending on their experience so far, but some will have a grasp of specialist terms from their personal areas of interest and exploration.
- Their knowledge is such that five-year-olds are now likely to recognise if they do not know a word, used by an adult or peer, and to ask for the meaning - so long, of course, that they feel confident in this setting.
- These, now slightly older, children have grasped some of the subtleties of spoken language. They often know that it is possible to create different meanings, and certainly to highlight a point, by placing strong emphasis on one or two words within a sentence.
- Five- and six-year-olds are beginning to be sensitive to different versions of spoken language, for instance, that you talk in a different way when speaking up in circle time from informal conversation with a peer or an adult.

- Five- and six-year-olds are more able to control and direct the volume of their spoken language, whereas younger children find it hard to speak quietly. However, some six- and seven-year-olds still struggle to recognise and adjust their volume.
- In order to master the sound system of the language, children need to be able to hear the words clearly and have plenty of practice in speaking, without being pressured to say words correctly. Help and encouragement means that most seven-year-olds will have mastered all the sounds they need.
- So, even when children are five or six years of age, a few problems with spoken sounds are not unusual, Most languages have some more difficult sounds or combinations. In English, the tough groups tend to include distinguishing the sounds made with the letters 's', 'f' and 'th' or 'r', 'l', 'w' and 'y'.
- Young children learn to speak a language and they generalise from the grammar rules they know so far. Even five- and six-year-olds struggle with the more complex rules, especially in a language like English, that has an exception to most (maybe all) rules. Speech and language specialists do not worry about children whose mistakes are logical. For instance, the standard pattern is big-bigger-biggest. However, it is incorrect to say bad-badder-baddest; the correct version is bad-worse-worst. Even if they have cracked that example, five-year-olds will still be making this sensible mistake for other non-standard word patterns of this kind.
- Five-year-olds and rising sixes can show a wide range in their use of language. They use descriptive comments and questions, speculate and wonder, explain, justify and occasionally argue.
- In relaxed conversation, five-year-olds (like many of the examples in *What Does it Mean to be Four?*) can use their listening and talking skills. Many children of this age have gained some understanding of the ground rules for talking and listening in group work, although they still find the turn taking hard sometimes.
- In order to gain an accurate idea of five-year-old skills of spoken language, it is important that adults listen and share in ordinary conversations and not only in the more structured exchanges of a busy adult-led group activity.
- Five-year-olds often still speak out loud in order to organise their thoughts or when they are tackling something new or difficult. With adult support and patience, many children are able to harness their language to express feelings and views, raise issues and undertake some problem-solving.

For example

At Poplar Play Centre there was plenty of social conversation around the lunch table. Children ate their lunch but there was relaxed time for chatting. Dessert was a bowl of orange and melon chunks, cut up into hand-held size. These were eaten with obvious enjoyment at all the tables - a clear message that children will happily eat fruit when it is given to them.

The five- to seven-year-olds (the holiday playscheme children) were on a table themselves and conversation ranged over a number of topics.

- Marcella (five years) queried Simone (five years), 'why did you put the melon in the water? To make lemon juice?' and Simone corrected with, 'no, melon juice'. Another child commented, 'you can't eat lemon' and Simone suggested, 'you can suck it'. The counter argument came with, 'lemon is too sour'.

Being a helpful adult

Many of the practical issues raised under communication in *What Does it Mean to be Four?* are still of direct relevance for being genuinely supportive of five-year-olds. In brief:

- Five-year-olds still take a strong lead from their familiar adults. Children are well able to listen as well as talk. But the five-year-olds, who are good at listening, have most usually experienced adults who show them the respect of listening.
- Five-year-olds have the potential to show a wide range of uses of language but much depends on their experience to date. They also need that the adults in their life show a range of use of language and do not, for instance, depend heavily on a questioning style, especially questions to which adults already know the answer.

- The children had a busy discussion about the details of a game for later. It sounded like a fantasy pretend game and there was much talk of who would take which character. There was serious discussion about who would be a 'baddy' and a 'goody' and how many baddies and goodies they needed. There was a conversation about why it was better to be one role rather than the other. Damian (five years old) explained at length about a character called Piccolo and narratives from what sounded like a video or cartoon series. He wanted to explain in detail about scenes in which the characters change hair.
- Another discussion unfolded about what would happen about school when the holidays were over (it was early August at the time). Several children spoke up about the class they would then be joining. Children had different ways of describing their transition: 'I'll be in Year 1', 'I'm going into Class 2' and 'I'm in Stage 1'. Questions flowed about which school other children attended. Yasmin (seven years old) explained to other children about the school she knew and how the Infants was downstairs and the Juniors upstairs. Some of the children attended her school and she seemed to be explaining what they were to expect.

Communication in groups: using circle time

The idea of circle time developed for children in primary school but the idea can be carefully adjusted for slightly younger children. Circle time operates as a carefully planned small group time to explore issues and ideas with children in a supportive way. However, it only works when the adult is sensitive and responsive to the events of the group that day.

Originally, a high priority in using circle time was for children to learn to listen supportively to each other and experience the same respect in return. The circle time depended on children feeling that they had the full support and respect of the adult. Some work using circle time continues to operate in this positive way, but there are concerns about an unreflective use of a general group time.

For example

Small group time, whether it is called circle time or not, can be an opportunity for adults to raise issues with children as a means to explain what is happening. I have known early years practitioners carefully raise issues about adjustments that will be made in anticipation of the arrival of a disabled child. I have also known a respectful explanation of why the ground rules are allowed to be flexible to support a child whose behaviour is challenging. Sensitive adults are able to tune into five-year-old understanding that allows them to tolerate some variation for a good reason.

Circle time can work so long as there is a considered balance between the session plan and what children want to say on the topic.

- Adults need to enable all the children, ideally, to take part but not press them. Five-year-olds can learn about social and emotional issues, if their own perspective is recognised. They will not learn to be more aware of the perspective of others or to listen, just because an adult has completed today's session plan for the circle time slot.
- Effective circle time means that power and direction is shared between adult and children. Such a balance is difficult for some adults, especially if they work within a setting in which daily practice does not invite children's views, whatever the claims in principle about listening or consultation.

- Adults who lead circle time need to have learned a range of group skills. For instance, confidentiality can be an issue, since children who are comfortable in circle time may share personal family issues in public, because it does not feel public to them. Sensitive circle time leaders need to show children that they have been heard, yet gently bring an end to that strand of talk if it is a private family matter.

Hilary Cremin has explored the running of circle time in some primary schools. To work well, circle time needs to be well integrated as a valued part of Personal, Social and Health Education (PSHE) within the curriculum, as a positive approach to children's behaviour and genuine consultation. She stresses that the adult needs to feel confident in dealing respectfully with the process of discussion within a group. They also need to avoid heavy reliance on the session plan, regardless of the evidence from children's behaviour that they would be motivated by one direction for discussion rather than another. From her observations, Hilary Cremin pointed to the negative impact of lack of connection between ideas being discussed and actual events happening within circle time itself. One example she gives is that of a teacher asking children to share in the group how they felt about bullying. Yet this adult seemed unaware that one individual child was being bullied at this same time by peers. The other children wiped the talking object after this girl had held it for the reason that otherwise they would catch her germs.

Thinking and expressing opinions

In the few years since the first edition of this book, it has become very common that children and young people are asked for their opinion through consultation exercises, some on a national level. Thoughtful early years and school teams have for some time explored the possibilities of consultation with children about daily life, problem solving on situations that affect everyone and planned changes for the school environment, most usually the outdoors space. Such teams mobilise the thinking skills of even the youngest children in provision on school grounds.

Some practical consultation projects with children aged from three to five were described in *What Does it Mean to be Four?*, page 14. Consultation with children has been developed within some primary schools and this development can be a powerful vehicle for five-year-olds' language for thinking. When the process works well, consultation is part of a reflective approach by the school team, including a positive approach to children's behaviour and integrated into the PSHE programme for Year 1 onwards. Five- and six-year-olds can already be aware of adults who pretend to ask for children's views and then take no notice. `So over-sixes can be observant, and scathing, about inauthentic consultation.

In primary schools it is as important as in early years (or out-of-school care settings) that adults think about what they mean and how they will develop the consultation process.

- Be clear about what you want to ask children and the boundaries to any discussion. If there are non-negotiable issues, then be honest with children.
- Think about how you present a discussion on which the children can have genuine input. For instance, when children are consulted about developing the school grounds, the discussion starts more constructively when children are asked what they want to be able to do in break time. Learning Through Landscapes (www.ltl.org. uk) describe this sensible focus on possibilities for play, rather than

Food for thought

These are the learning outcomes for *Communication and Language* within *The Curriculum framework for children 3-5* that applies in Scotland. It is expected that five-year-olds will be able to :

- Use books to find interesting information
- Recognise the link between the written and spoken word
- Understand some of the language and layout of books
- Develop an awareness of letter names and sounds in the context of play experiences
- Use their own drawings and written marks to express feelings and ideas
- Experiment with symbols, letters and in some cases words in writing
- Recognise some familiar words and letters, for example the initial letter in their name

inviting a wish list for equipment. If children are keen for opportunities to climb and clamber, there are more ways of meeting this request that the purchase of fixed climbing equipment.

- With this kind of starter question, you are then more likely to sort out problems that need resolving with the children, rather than rushing straight to solutions. Perhaps they want somewhere to sit protected from the cold in winter and the sun in summer, there needs to be space for football and why do the playground staff keep telling us to get off the flower bed edges when they are ideal for practising our balancing?
- Every issue is not up for discussion. You can still show respect for children by telling them about a decision made by the adults, giving an explanation appropriate to their understanding and answering any questions.
- You need to consider what the children have said and how their views will be taken into account. If children cannot see in what ways their views have made a difference, then they will lose enthusiasm for giving their ideas.

For example

The Save the Children consultation project, led by Lina Farjerman, describes case studies featuring children of different ages. One example shows the competence of five-year-olds in an out-of-school situation. The Birmingham Young Volunteers Adventure Camps wanted to find ways to involve younger children – five-, six- and seven-year-olds - in the planning of their own holiday. The children used a pictorial food questionnaire to identify liked and disliked foods. The menu was then planned around children's preferences. As a result, there was less wastage of food but

Early Years Foundation Stage strands -

Linking sounds and letters
- Hear and say sounds in words in the order in which they occur
- Link sounds to letters, naming and sounding the letters of the alphabet *
- Use their phonic knowledge to write simple regular words and make phonetically plausible attempts at more complex words* ®

Reading
- Explore and experiment with sounds, words and texts
- Retell narratives in the correct sequence, drawing on language patterns of stories
- Read a range of familiar and common words and simple sentences independently *
- Know that print carries meaning and, in English, is read from left to right and top to bottom
- Show an understanding of the elements of stories, such as main character, sequence of events and openings and how information can be found in non-fiction texts to answer questions about where, who, why and how

Writing
- Use their phonic knowledge to write simple regular words and make phonetically plausible attempts at more complex words *®
- Attempt writing for different purposes, using features of different forms such as lists, stories and instructions
- Write their own names and other things such as labels and captions and begin to form simple sentences, sometimes using punctuation*®

Handwriting
- Use a pencil and hold it effectively to form recognisable letters, most of which are correctly formed *

also the children started to trust the playworkers. During the holiday week the children were able to suggest activities, rather than follow a pre-determined schedule. They made some decisions about how money was spent and kept a daily diary that became their memento of the holiday.

Early literacy skills and five-year-olds

Early years practitioners working with fives will, of course, keep a close eye on the early learning goals over children's final year within the Early Years Foundation Stage. There should still be no rush – and practitioners need to keep well in mind that there is a significant difference in months of experience between the eldest and the youngest in a reception class. The majority of the goals will not cause undue problems, so long as they follow sensible interpretations of what this skill will look like in the world of a five-year-old. However, many of the ELGs about reading, writing and handwriting are not developmentally realistic expectations. They were imposed on the Foundation Stage through the national literacy strategy for primary schools. Nothing has changed, in terms of normal child development, to make them any more realistic, now that they have continued effectively unchanged into the EYFS.

Five-year-olds and rising sixes can have gained a strong understanding of written communication and they have started the process of being able to write and read. It is a realistic expectation that, by the end of the EYFS, most children will have the first building blocks of written language, the very beginnings of reading and writing. However, the starred (*) early learning goals in the box are not realistic expectations for most children to have achieved while they are still five years of age, and sometimes still young fives at the end of their EYFS. Even those five-year-olds whose achievements are striking for their age, will not be making the very low level of mistakes implied by the starred goals. In terms of child development, these goals are more realistic if applied to 'most' older sixes or seven-year-olds. Two goals are under review (2008) and these are marked by ® in the box opposite.

The EYFS was required to integrate the recommendation of the 2006 Rose Report that a structured programme of synthetics phonics should be started with children 'by the age of five' (not at some time during the year that children are five). The report also stresses the importance of speaking and listening skills but the overall import has been to consolidate the unrealistic expectations. The risk has been increased that, in order to try to get five-year-olds to reach unrealistic literacy targets, even more four-year-olds will be given formal reading and writing activities. Far from promoting early literacy, such pressure is more likely to disrupt children's learning. I appreciate the unenviable situation in which many practitioners and advisors now find themselves. But this a responsible book about child development and I am not going to agree that official targets are realistic expectations when they definitely are not.

This section of the book describes more realistic aims, drawing on child development and the helpful input of many reception practitioners, with whom I have spoken. Children are not dramatically different across the UK, so it can help English reception teams to realise that there are more realistic reading and writing learning outcomes in the curriculum guidance of Scotland and Wales (see the two Food for Thought boxes.)

Literacy is not simply discovered through unstructured experience. Reading and writing need to be made explicit, explained and modelled for children The development of literacy requires direct teaching; it does not just happen. The developmental concerns that are currently raised by early years specialists like myself are not about the need to teach children to read and write. The objection is to methods that require a very structured approach to start effectively with four-year-olds and gain serious momentum with young five-year-olds. Secure literacy needs direct instruction (and phonics) but this development can only work if what children are asked to do makes sense to them and connects to their current understanding.

Writing is a related yet different task from reading. Anne Hughes and Sue Ellis offer some useful questions for adults to consider in order to tune into the current understanding of individual children: what they understand so far about print as well as their technical skills for writing. I have woven in my own comments to their practical and helpful questions. Alert practitioners need to use their skills of observation to learn about individual children and their progress along the route to confident reading and writing.

- Does this individual child know the difference between words, letters and logos? All these seem very obviously different to us, but the distinctions have to be learned. Some five-year-olds who look very perplexed may not have yet discovered that there are separate number and letter systems.
- Does the child produce marks that look like writing, does he or she say it is 'writing' and says something in particular?
- What does this show about the child's understanding of letter formation and how writing looks different from drawing?
- Does the child always write in the correct direction for his or her language: from left to right in English. Are practitioners aware of a child's home language, the script and direction in which that is written?
- Does the child yet write any particular letters or words? If so, then it is worth understanding as an adult why these letters or whole words have meaning for the individual child.
- Can children copy letters or words: by copying over the top, from a piece of paper in front of them, from looking at writing on the walls?
- How does the child hold a pencil? Is it always in the same way, in the same hand? If children are left handed, then special materials may help them to see what they are doing.
- What letters can children reliably recognise? Can they recognise the first letter of their name? This word should be significant to them.
- Which letters do they sound out and do they know that the letters in their name make the sounds in their name?
- Can they find words and letters they need and then use them or do they always look to an adult to provide the word or letter?

Developmentally realistic expectations

Five-year-olds will vary but, with supportive and developmentally appropriate experiences of early literacy, the following are realistic expectations:

- Children can enjoy books and stories, having a good grasp of how stories and books work. Five-year-olds will have favourites and be able to express opinions about what makes a good book or a story.
- Children can show great enthusiasm for information (non-fiction) books and have learned that books are one way to find out about topics of interest. Some five-year-olds can be motivated to pursue their own interests using books as one resource.
- Children are likely to recognise some familiar words, including their own name, and public writing, like shop names.

Four- and five-year-olds are in the process of understanding what it means to be a reader or a writer. Their attitudes towards these skills and grasping what is real reading and writing are as much part of their learning as the technical skills. Penny Munn interviewed children about their understanding of reading several times during their final year before moving into primary school. She found that children's behaviour towards books did not alter much, but their beliefs about the process of reading were undergoing change. The main shift was from believing that reading was the same as turning pages and telling a story to the more accurate recognition that the process involved decoding print. Many children had then grasped that they could not yet read; it was something they now needed to learn. (See also *What Does it Mean to be Four?* page 34 for a description of Penny Munn's research.)

- Five-year-olds can have worked out that there is a written form of language as well as spoken. In diverse neighbourhoods they may have a clear understanding that different groups use visually different forms of writing.
- Many five-year-olds will have a good idea about writing, its form and shape and will be making a good attempt at many letters. (But it is not realistic to expect all five-year-olds to have good pencil control and form most of their letters correctly.)
- Five-year-olds can be enthusiastic mark makers, using their emergent writing skills, telling you what their writing 'says' and confidently using adults (practitioners and parents) to scribe for them.
- They are likely to write a small range of simple words. Some five-year-olds will have a good try at unfamiliar or more complex words by sound, but there is great variety. The risk of the relevant Early Learning Goal for this skill area is the impression it gives that most five-year-olds will be able to write a lot of words, mainly correctly.

Five-year-olds can have grasped that reading and writing are practical skills that can be used for different purposes. They need this understanding of the practical applications of written communication in order to motivate their own learning. If five-year-olds, and younger children, are pushed on too fast towards early reading and writing, there is a high risk they will believe they do their literacy work only because adults require it, rather than because the skills will be valuable to them. This negative outlook has been described as the risk that pressurised young children will learn to read, or write, in order to stop reading and writing. The children will believe that, once they have the skills, then adults will stop nagging them. Such an outlook is far removed from the positive disposition to learn that is so crucial for children's continued development.

There are serious risks for future learning if children are switched off the task of reading at an early age. I have appreciated conversations with specialists like Ros Bayley who works to help children whose enthusiasm for literacy has been stunted at an early stage. Ros Bayley has successfully motivated six- and seven-year-olds (often boys), who have decided

they are useless at reading, by coming in through stories set to a rap beat. (*Maurice the Mouse* and other stories are available from www.educationalpublications.com)

For example

There is no doubt that many five-year-olds have an impressive raft of early literacy skills. The serious concerns that I express in this section arise because unrealistic expectations, adrift from reliable child development knowledge, risk undervaluing the actual achievements of young children. If practitioners, and parents, are expecting far too much, then five-year-old skills will never be judged quite good enough.

I definitely recommend Robin Campbell's detailed account of the literacy development of his granddaughter, Alice. There is a clear description of Alice's well established literacy skills in the few months following her fifth birthday. This kind of account usefully shows the extent to which a child's confidence builds on a firm basis of happy early literacy experiences. However, Alice's skills are an important reminder about a realistic interpretation of those early learning goals for reading and handwriting. Alice has definitely joined the world of written language and she knows a great deal about how books work. However, at just over five years of age – when some children complete their time in the EYFS - she still makes many mistakes in reading and writing.

The great importance of oral communication

Effective practice with five-year-olds has to value oral communication. Children cannot tune into the sounds of their language without a rich experience of conversation, songs and rhymes. But talking is also a vital part of building writing skills. Many Reception practitioners, with whom I have spoken, are clear about the importance of oral communication. But they share the concern that there can be serious difficulties in holding to what they know to be developmentally sound, when they experience pressure to move the children on quickly towards written communication skills.

Practitioners need to model for children how they can talk about what they will write, that using language for thinking and planning is the step before writing, or getting an adult to scribe for you. Five-year-olds need to gain the understanding that talking is a way of organising your thoughts, how to raise and play around with possible ideas and consider a story line. Oral communication is also the vehicle for exploring and deciding what kind of writing is needed for this task, for instance is the aim to inform, describe, instruct, direct?

For example

There are examples of good practice from Reception, Years 1 and 2. I was told one reassuring anecdote by a Foundation Stage adviser (in Sheffield) of a Year 2 teacher who fully recognised the link between oral communication, play and writing skills.

The lesson plan for the day was that the children would write about islands. The teacher quickly realised that the children were confused about what an island was. Wisely, instead of continuing with the plan, she organised for the children to spend time that afternoon in the nursery. They made islands in the sand and water trays, talked about them, understood what made an island and what might be on an island. The children then returned to their classroom full of ideas and ready to talk, plan and, finally, write.

The crucial role of oral language is recognised in most of the official documents about building literacy skills, including the Rose Report. However, there is a disruptive, combined effect of the unrealistic early learning goals for much of literacy and a pressure on practitioners to move children's learning along at a brisk pace. Prior to the development of the EYFS, the SPRINT project (Study of Primary Interactive Teaching) explored some of the consequences for reception, year 1 and 2 teams. The team showed how the requirements of the National Literacy Strategy (for England) had created difficulties in implementation: that quality of work with children is incompatible with the demand that teaching must be 'well paced with a sense of urgency' (a specific phrase from the strategy).

Even the most experienced practitioners cannot resolve these twin demands; high quality oral work with children is incompatible with a sense of pressure and urgency. It is also appropriate to challenge why there must be 'a sense of urgency' . The risk becomes that practitioners can behave as if the most important goal is to complete the lesson plan, rather than that the children have demonstrably understood what is covered in the plan. The SPRINT team noted that, under pressure, oral communication can easily become weighted towards a high level of adult questioning. In one-way, directive communication, children's replies to adult questions were short - less than 5 per cent of the children's answers were more than ten words long.

Five-year-olds learn through doing, talking and thinking. Helpful adults can support that process by their own use of language as well as the ways in which they organise the learning environment. The EPPE project (see also page 6) highlighted the importance of adult-child interactions and a process of 'sustained shared thinking'. Although five-year-olds can learn during small group activity, they are still best oriented to one-to-one interaction or very small groups indeed. The adult-child ratio in Reception classes is not ideal, but five-year-olds do not spend all their time in school. The input of the Reception team is important but partnership with parents can communicate how much children can learn through relaxed conversation at home.

For example

In Sun Hill Reception class the team focus on following children's interests and chosen conversations. Adults are easily available, both indoors and outside, to chat with children: to listen comments and respond to questions that children want to ask right now. Flexible topic planning is shaped by searching questions voiced by individual chIdren. During small group times children are invited to say what they feel they have learned today. Their own evaluations lead to questions from other children and open-ended 'I wonder...' questions from the adult.

Supporting children's learning requires a reflective approach to adult language and use of language. It is worth considering:

- Do you set a good example to show the social and communication skills of a genuine conversation?
- Open-ended questions are an important part of what the REPEY team call sustained shared thinking. But questions, even open-ended ones, can be over used. What sort of questions are you asking?

- What are children learning? Partly, they have ideas about what adults want of them in this setting.
- If children perceive that their role is to answer questions, they may cease to bother to use their rich range of language with this adult or in this setting.
- Do you listen as well as talk? Can children hear that your reply has built on what they said?
- What happens when you do not understand a child? Do you ask for a repetition or say 'pardon'? Do you actually say, 'I don't understand what you're saying?' Unless you do, then children often do not realise that an adult is confused.
- What happens when children do not understand you and in what ways may they show it? Do they look puzzled or blank, give the wrong or an odd answer, stay silent or try distractions?
- Do you keep going or stop? Do you bring the issue to the fore with, 'you look puzzled' or 'that's an interesting answer; what makes you say that?' or 'do you understand what I'm asking?'
- Do you model the useful ways to show in words the difference between not hearing something, and requesting a repetition, and not understanding, in which case repetition does not help.

Children also need to think and plan what they will write. Writing is also about composition; Penny Tassoni explains in her presentations that simply copying writing, however correctly, does not make anyone into a real writer. Children need their secure skills of oral communication to feel confident in talking through their plans and being clear about how to tell a story, when their current plan is to write one down on paper. Jane Ginsborg and Ann Locke focus on the serious consequences for literacy when young children are not given generous time for talking and listening over early childhood. Practitioners, and parents, who are anxious to get children on to 'proper' reading and writing, are likely to disrupt the oral language skills upon which the literacy skills depend.

How do writing skills develop for children?

There will be great variety in writing skills and it is important to recall how children move towards being writers.

- Young children, some as young as three years old, produce wavy streams across the page in a fairly level line that they will tell you are 'my writing'. They have grasped that people write and that writing looks different from drawing.
- They tend to move on to 'scribble' script where the continuous wavy lines now have some gaps and the wave form has become more varied.
- Once children has grasped that writing is made up of different symbols, what they call their writing moves to being separate marks, some of which begin to look like letters. Perhaps the children tell you that a given mark is a letter. The letter shapes are then sometimes grouped together in word-like clusters
- Children know what some letters look like and that important words, such as their name, are represented by the same set of symbols/letters each time. They want to write a word that is familiar and of significance to them.
- Children start to have a go at a set of words to say something deliberately. They have a growing awareness of letters and some words, also that written words have a practical use, such as conveying a message.

Learning to be a writer is tough for children, even harder than learning to read. As well as all the decoding skills that children need as a reader, they have to form the letters as a writer. Children also need to think and plan what they will write.

Children need to feel that they are treated as writers, at the same time that adults are helping them with all the technical details of learning to write. Five-year-olds have a great deal of practice ahead of them and their motivation can be supported by adults who show that writing is useful, in all kinds of ways it gets results.

Five-year-olds will begin to use their emerging writing skills for different purposes. But they also need to see adults model what it is like to be a writer and that writing can work in different ways. In order to extend children's understanding, it can be helpful if adults (parents as well as practitioners) sometimes explain out loud what they are doing and why. Writing something can support different intentions, to:

- Communicate to other people - a message, notice, request
- Organise your thoughts - ideas, plan of actions
- Ensure that the writer does not forget something - sticky notes, reminder notes to oneself, shopping lists

Writing for different purposes looks different and some five-year-olds have the experience to recognise that writing formats differ. For instance, letters look different from shopping lists, an information notice stuck to the board looks different from a diary or a practitioner's observation notes.

A partnership with parents is essential in supporting children's early literacy. Penny Munn reported that children who were familiar with books from home and who had experienced helpful adults were less daunted by the prospect of having to learn to read. Children whose families had not provided a home literacy experience, tended to be far less confident. Five-year-olds need to see writing in a practical context as a useful skill that can be used in all sorts of applications and not as something you do because 'teachers' want you to complete writing activities. Partnership with parents is important to explain and show, if parents are doubtful, how much children learn through practical writing and reading within the family.

Cathy Nutbrown's Raising Early Achievement in Literacy (REAL) project in Sheffield identified four main strands of literacy in working together with parents, some of whom were uncertain of their abilities in this area, or felt that literacy was a task for the experts. Dorothy Caddell shows similar strands in her descriptions of partnership in early years settings in Scotland. Part of the encouragement to parents can be the recognition of how much they are already doing with their children. In terms of literacy:

- Adults need to encourage children in their awareness of environmental print: that writing is all around us and used in everyday life.
- Parents make a considerable contribution when they use and enjoy books with their children, as part of an enjoyable shared time together.
- Family routines offer many opportunities to show how writing is a practical skill, to involve children and let them observe how familiar adults use their writing skills.
- Parents are well placed to promote phonological awareness for children through song and nursery rhymes.

Problem Solving, Reasoning and Numeracy

The EYFS has changed the heading of this area of learning from 'Mathematical Development', but the Early Learning Goals are the same as in the Foundation Stage guidance. In contrast with some of the goals about literacy, these expectations for early mathematical understanding are developmentally realistic for most five-year-olds, by the end of the EYFS. Potential problems in practice can arise if practitioners focus too much on the abstract side of number. Fives still need a meaningful context for their application of mathematics, but research has identified that young children are powerful mathematical thinkers. It is useful to note that there is no expectation that most fives will be able to write their numbers – an interesting contrast with the expectations required for young children and their letters!

Five-year-olds still need a meaningful context for their application of mathematics, but research has identified that young children are powerful mathematical thinkers.

Early Years Foundation Stage strand

- Numbers as labels and for counting
- Say and use number names in order in familiar contexts
- Count reliably up to ten everyday objects
- Recognise numerals 1 to 9
- Use developing mathematical ideas and methods to solve practical problems

Children's early mathematical thinking

The ideas of Jean Piaget have had a significant influence on early years practice in the UK. But his research took a narrow focus on the ways in which children younger than six years were able to think, including their understanding of mathematical concepts. Piaget's experiments worked at a level of abstraction that made limited sense to four- and five-year-olds and his interpretations were biased towards what children did not understand rather than what they could grasp. The practical application of Piaget's ideas has been strongly challenged.

The work of Margaret Donaldson, and her team in Edinburgh in the 1970s (now spread around the UK), established a more flexible approach to research. Five-year-olds emerge as powerful mathematical thinkers, so long as they are enabled to make connections with the environment and ideas they already know.

Piaget's argument was that children must understand the principle of conservation before they can develop the concept of number. Children have learned to conserve number when they agree that the number of objects remains the same even when they are moved to look different, for instance a row is pushed together or spread. The practical application of Piaget's claims was that five-year-olds could not really understand counting, so their enthusiastic 'counting up to' skills, often encouraged by parents, were meaningless and 'just rote learning'. This stance is no longer justifiable.

In Piaget's experiments, children under five or six years would usually say that there were less items when a row of toys had been pushed closer together. However, studies by Margaret Donaldson's team showed that children were responsive to the details of the experiment. They were far more likely to be confident that two rows of the same number of toys were still the same when a soft toy, Naughty Teddy, pushed one row up tighter, than when the adult had brought about the same change. The children had a good grasp of number and the confusion seemed to arise when adults asked the question, 'are they the same?', when it was the adult who did the moving. Children are active thinkers and many of them try to cooperate with adults who ask questions, even if the question seems a bit odd. The children's logic seemed to be that something must have changed as a result of the adult action, otherwise why was this adult asking the question. Naughty Teddy did not bring in this source of confusion.

Learning about counting

Five-year-olds can be capable and counting is an important activity for children. There is a strong link of understanding that builds between children's counting, for practical reasons as well as sheer pleasure, and their growing understanding of the written system of number.

- Some four-year-olds are reliable counters but some get confused within the counting process. Five-year-olds are more adept, and often very confident, as they co-ordinate the words and touch as part of counting to a purpose.
- Five- and six-year-olds are more able to start counting from any point in the number sequence. Since they are confident with the number order, they are far more likely to be able to count on from a given number. When children are younger, they have

to say the sequence from one onwards. Understanding order enables children to use counting on strategies.

- There is an overlapping pattern of development that involves verbal skills (the number words), physical development (the touching and moving of objects) and thinking skills as children grasp some of the abstract aspects related to the number task.

Penny Munn spent time talking individually with children during their last year in nursery and their first term of primary school. On each of four visits she asked the children the same basic questions including 'can you count?' and 'Why do you count?' In this way Penny Munn highlighted children's beliefs about counting, in much the same way as her research on reading (see *What Does it Mean to be Four?* page 39).

- Four-year-olds started out by believing that counting was the same as saying the number words - rather like they believed that reading was the same as re-telling the story.
- Many four-year-olds were perplexed by the question 'why do you count?' They did not understand, and had not been shown through adult actions that you count to know how many.
- It was rare for young children to understand the adult purpose of counting until they went to school. Then, more and more they began to realise that we count 'to know how many'.
- The four-year-olds, in nursery, seemed to view counting much more as a playful and social activity. Perhaps this perspective is unsurprising, since the children tended to experience counting as part of songs and games like hide and seek. Adults were usually the ones who kept score or made a tally.

Adults, practitioners and parents often assume that their purposes in doing something are clear to children. But they are not. Penny Munn points out that children are helped when adults make their purpose in counting clear to children. Adults need to create a link between the numbers and a practical task, such as to see how many children are here for lunch or work out that the group is two overalls short. Counting, like many mathematical activities for children, is a technical skill but also needs a context. Children need to have a sensible reason to practise and use the skill that answers the questions of 'how many' or 'are they the same?' Penny Munn's research is especially useful, because it opens the door to five-year-old thinking and shows that helpful practitioners can be more obvious about why they count. Then it is clearer to children that we count to know how many: how many items we have and how many we need – perhaps because we are short of some. Penny Munn has shown that children need to grasp the purpose of counting and then fours and fives become more active in using counting to solve practical problems.

The practical applications of recent research for mathematical thinking are that:

- Early years practitioners need to recognise that five-year-olds are capable of a great deal of mathematical thinking, so long as they can make connections to what is familiar to them in routines, practical tasks and activities.
- You need to be ready to explore what five-year-olds know already. In this age group, there can be a wide variety of current knowledge and understanding, depending on the children's previous experience.
- Number and other mathematical ideas start to make sense to children because they apply the ideas in a practical context. Pretend play, construction activities and many domestic routines, at home as well as in the Reception class, give a firm grounding to maths.

- Five-year-olds are helped when adults voice their own mathematical actions and thinking out loud. In much the same way as bringing writing alive, adults need to make their maths explicit to children: what they are doing by counting or measuring and to what end(s).
- Saying it out loud is a useful discipline for adults. It can also address the potential problems caused by adults assuming that what is obvious to them must also be obvious to five-year-olds - often not the case.
- Early numeracy, just like early literacy, has to be interactive, so that children are able to get involved with materials that they can move around and not be restricted to worksheets. Children need to engage by actions and words with their peers and with interested adults.

Early Years Foundation Stage strand -

Calculating
- In practical activities and discussion begin to use the vocabulary involved in adding and subtracting
- Use language such as 'more' or 'less' to compare two numbers
- Find one more or one less than a number from one to ten
- Begin to relate addition to combining two groups of objects and subtraction to 'taking away'

Adult thinking; child thinking

Five-year-olds have grasped many of the ideas that perplex four-year-olds and simply pass by three-year-olds. Those much younger children have not yet gained the experience in which to embed and make any sense of the ideas. But five-year-olds are still young children. If all has gone well, they are keen to learn and not too daunted by the prospect of not knowing something or feeling confused at the outset. Their experiences now, in Reception class, and for some in Year 1 of school, are crucial.

- Five-year-olds know many numbers and a counting order. They will recognise some numbers written down and used in different ways.
- They can handle some of the more abstract ideas in which numbers are used in mathematical operations such as adding and subtraction.
- They also have the beginnings of the idea of dividing up quantities in terms of sharing out into equal numbers or amounts. This type of division makes sense to five-year-olds and their concern for fairness.

Careful observation of five-year-olds shows that they can be confused if adults do not connect abstract ideas clearly to a familiar context. Penny Munn and her colleagues in Strathclyde have explored teacher behaviour with regard to five-year-olds and maths. Their findings, and the practical applications, are of direct relevance anywhere in the UK and reflective practitioners can find links to supporting children's learning across all the areas. Following observations of teachers with fives and young sixes, the team noticed that some practitioners struggled on with their mathematical lesson plan, although it seemed very obvious that the children were perplexed about what their teacher was asking and what they were supposed to do. It became clear that adult strategies had to include the reflection of 'are we talking about the same thing?' This phrase is deceptively simple and very important. Practitioners need to act differently if the answer is 'no', the children and adult are not talking about the same thing at all.

Another way of describing what happens, as Penny Munn and her colleagues outline, is the difference between 'shared reference' (adults and children are talking about the same thing) and 'non-shared reference' (talking about something different). This distinction can arise in other areas of learning besides early mathematical understanding. For instance, it is possible to be deep in conversation with a five-year-old about the natural world or how our bodies work (Knowledge and Understanding of the World). Then you realise that the child is missing a significant piece of information and is confused. Alternatively, a four- or five-year-old has made the assumption that adults know what children know - but you are ignorant of facts that feel obvious to this child.

Non-shared reference is not a problem so long as the adult recognises the impasse, stops the flow of adult talk, asks open questions and listens. Adults can then explain properly, because they have now grasped what it is that the children do not understand. It is unwise to press on with an adult-led activity, even though children are confused and giving 'odd' answers, from the perspective of adult knowledge. In mathematical understanding, just as in any other area of learning, there are serious risks if adults feel that the main objective is to cover the curriculum plan for today, rather than to ensure that children really have understood the key ideas. As illogical as it sounds, anxious adults do behave as if completion of the required plan for the day ensures that children have learned within the written, planned objectives. Unfortunately such an approach risks creating a situation in which five- and six-year-olds resign themselves to a sense of confusion, of not knowing, and feel increasingly that this emotion will be part of their school experience.

Time given to ensure they understand and to check you are talking about the same thing is invaluable, not an optional extra. There is no point in going on if the children do not understand. They have not learned the concept; they have learned that maths (or whatever) is confusing and you just have to put up with not understanding.

Children need a considerable amount of practice in using mathematical ideas and handling numbers and number operations. There is no point in rushing children on to new ideas if they have not yet consolidated their existing concepts. Dorothy Caddell points out that, compared with the UK, approaches to teaching maths in other European countries place a far stronger focus on time for practice.

- Textbooks from mainland Europe work on the pattern that three to five times as much learning time should be spent on practice and consolidation as on the introduction of concepts in the first place. It is unhelpful to children if practitioners move them on when they have only just grasped a concept.
- There is less variation in the look of mathematical exercises. More recent traditions in the UK have emphasised having a lot of variety in activities for children. The logical reasoning behind practice in much of mainland Europe is that young children get distracted from the core mathematical idea when the task in front of them looks too different.
- I would add that the expressed goal in the UK has too often been that 'maths should be fun!' To be frank, most children would give up on the fun and opt for

understanding and feeling confident through practice. We want children to find early mathematical experiences of interest and to provide enough of a challenge to stimulate, without being too difficult.

- Arithmetic on mainland Europe is given a strong weighting. Younger school children are given relatively more practice with handling numbers in their head (mental arithmetic) than paper and pencil calculations.

Mathematical language and thinking

A well-resourced indoor and outdoor learning environment will provide many opportunities for fives to use their mathematical skills of measuring, estimating, and counting. When practitioners listen in to children, they often realise that sophisticated (five-year-old level) and practical maths is happening within child-initiated play and conversation. There is no need to plan adult-initiated or adult-led activities when such learning is fully supported by spontaneous play.

A valuable example is provided by Joy Roberts, who undertook research into learning through play in reception classes and described that practitioners sometimes did not trust the power of play. From her own experience as a reception teacher, she recognised how easy it could be to take that wrong turn. She recalled a time when she had prepared an activity sheet about position and assessed children's understanding through their worksheet and response to her questions. Later in the same day, she listened to the very same children playing with their vehicles. Their spontaneous play language was full of terms about spatial position, the order of the cars as they were raced, degrees of speed, size and shape. It was perfectly possible to assess the children's rich understanding in this area of learning through their freely chosen play. Mathematical thinking and practical application can benefit from the support of adult-initiated experiences, some of which may at the start be adult-led. But these experiences will never be best organised around lots of pre-prepared worksheets. The best experiences and linked activities stretch over time. A good example is given by Liz Marsden

and Jenny Woodbridge, who describe the absorbing games project undertaken by teacher, Lesley Hill, with some of her reception class children. Five-year-old girls and boys became fully involved in playing a game dependent on understanding numbers and then creating their own games. The children were able, and keen, to talk about their games: how they worked, what was interesting. They were also enthusiastic about reflecting on what they felt that had learned at different stages of the project – and showed an accurate memory of earlier stages of the games project.

Five-year-olds will show that they understand an impressive range of abstract ideas that have mathematical connections. They can handle many of these concepts through explanation, discussion and thinking out loud with words. But five-year-olds often still need a familiar context and the sense created by practical application:

- Five-year-olds are likely to be able to handle a wide range of sorting and matching tasks, because they have a sound grasp of same and different on many dimensions.
- They can handle simple ideas of practical measurement of quantities, the ideas of more, less and just enough. Their skills of comparison and of judging same and different can be sharp, so long as the context is familiar.
- Ideas of relative size, weight and shape make sense to five-year-olds and their vocabulary will have extended to be more precise about 'bigness': tall and short, taller than, heavy and light, and the different words used to describe shapes.

Some mathematical ideas, that seem basic and obvious to adults, can still confuse five-year-olds:

- The concepts of distance, speed and time can become confused. Five-year-olds try to work out that how long it takes to get somewhere is only partly about how far away is the destination. Mode of travel and delays affect the time of a journey.
- Five-year-olds can have a growing understanding of time passing, but telling the time in terms of clocks is still difficult and many six- and seven-year-olds will struggle.

Adults need to tune into the task of telling the time in order to realise that children have much to understand and that telling the time with confidence takes a lot of practice.

- Nowadays children have to negotiate understanding time from clocks with moving hands (analogue) and from the many digital timepieces that give only numbers (in a 12- or 24-hour system). Many domestic appliances and ICT give time in a digital format.
- The division of time into 60 minutes in an nour and 24 hours in the day is an arbitrary system. Children need to have grasped the number system and to understand that, with the exception of 24-hour clocks, the 12-hour system is repeated in a day.
- Clocks and watches with moving hands have to be understood on a 'big hand, little hand' basis. Then there is the confusing business of quarter past, half past and quarter to the hour.

An understanding of time is not exclusively mathematical – maths tends to focus on the measurement of time and accuracy about 'what's the time now?' Fives are also ready to extend their understanding of time and time passing, in a more 'historical' sense, and that is covered in the next section.

Five-year-olds understand and can voice the ideas of many positional concepts, but the difference between left and right orientation is still difficult. The problem is that children have to grasp that left/right seems to change from the perspective taken - 'my right hand is always this one but if I face my friend then her right hand seems to be on the other side'. So children need to be clear about what is their own right and left hand or side of the body.

You might like to reflect on how you managed to sort out left and right in your own chidhood. Most people, with whom I have spoken, managed to get one side 'fixed'. For example they knew they had a little scar on their left hand, so by elimination the other hand and side of the body had to be the right. I was motivated to get my rights andlefts very clear in order not to collide with my peers as we followed our teacher's verbal instructions during our country dancing sessions. How about you?

Knowledge and Understanding of the World

Five-year-olds, just like their younger selves, can be interested in the world around them, including the outdoor natural environment. Children can be enthusiastic learners. They can be keen and able to do simple research from information books and CD Roms. But they enjoy and really need direct access to the outdoors, experiencing the weather, natural materials like earth and mud, plants and small creatures. Four- and five-year-olds can be competent and involved gardeners in their outdoor space. They learn about the process of growth though direct action and are proud of what they have grown in their early years setting - to admire and sometimes to eat.

Early Years Foundation Stage strand - Exploration and investigation

* Investigate objects and material by using all of their senses as appropriate
* Find out about, and identify, some features of living things, objects and events they observe
* Look closely at similarities, differences, patterns and changes
* Ask questions about why things happen and how things work

Looking, listening and learning

Given choices and relaxed time, four- and five-year-olds can be keen observers and notice changes over time. There does not always have to be an end product, like a drawing, although sometimes children want to do such an activity. Children learn through observation, talking, thinking and recalling. They can also learn to use and take care of basic scientific tools, like a magnifying glass, binoculars, bug boxes and a camera. A relaxed approach to writing materials can also mean that children often choose to document their discoveries with writing, asking an adult to scribe, and using cameras.

Four- and five-year-olds are curious and this outlook is a firm foundation for a scientific outlook. They are keen to explore, wondering in words and actions, 'what will happen if ...?' - another building block to scientific thought. Helpful adults follow children's interests, even if they are at an angle to the plan for the day or session. Flexible planning allows for children's enthusiasm, so that they can spend more time on some aspects of exploration and less on others, if only for today. Children will explore through hands-on activity but also by their questions (see also *What Does it Mean to be Four?*, especially pages 44-46). Helpful adults help to build children's general knowledge and wish to explore and find out more.

Good practice means recognising the importance of children's questions. Children's questions and comments are not interrupting learning. On the contrary, they are the cutting edge of learning. Early years practitioners may need to reflect on the adult role they are taking, perhaps without clear and conscious decision. Practitioners may have childhood memories of teachers dealing swiftly with questions, or even becoming irritated because the questions took up too much time and 'we have to get on'. It is crucial that early years practitioners leave this image well behind them.

Another good reason is that, in recent years, good primary school practice has been influenced by some serious adult thinking about the ways in which children's thinking skills develop potentially – or can be blocked.

- The 1999 review by Carol McGuinness raised many practical issues about what happens to the development of thinking skills over middle childhood, if children are not given time and encouragement to ask their own questions, speculate and sometimes disagree with teachers.
- The project on independent learning, led by David Whitebread, raised similar issues from early years into the first years of primary school. The project reports point out, amongst other important issues, that children learned to wait for adult answers and direction, when they rarely had the time to discover for themselves – through direct active experience and putting their thoughts into spoken words.
(You can read more about these and other developments in my *Understanding children and young people: development from 5-18 years*.)

Of course, these ideas do not only apply to Knowledge and Understanding of the World - another reminder that young children's learning crosses all the boundaries. I chose to place this material here because over-structured adult planning, in some early years teams, has removed the excitement and learning potential of this aspect of development. In the introduction to *First hand experience: what matters to children* the team of early years and primary specialists explain the observations that led to developing this resource (see reference under Diane Rich on page 72). They describe second-hand activities such as a lesson plan for five-year-olds on taste in which there was nothing real to eat and adult-led activities about pets that were supported only by images downloaded from the internet.

Children need authentic experiences to make sense of their world and to fire up their thinking and communicative skills. Such experiences can be offered within a topic-based approach to planning, but not if everything is pre-packaged. The materials for the EYFS also confirm what has always been the situation for the Foundation Stage. Flexible planning through topics is one way of looking ahead. But the method is not compulsory and nor does it work unless open-ended adult plans are very responsive – in timing, content and short-term final planning - to the actual interests and knowledge of young children.

The REPEY project, led by Iram Siraj-Blatchford, explored the pattern of supportive adult communication in twelve settings that had been identified, in the main EPPE project, has having good practice. The research report (see page 72) provides many examples of how fours and fives are able to use their language skills to explore their knowledge and understanding of their world. My particular favourite is a flowing, and occasionally argumentative, conversation between a boy and girl, who were approaching five years of age. They have a lively discussion, whilst being busy with their drawing, about bones and blood in the human body, led through their different perspectives on how God makes bodies. Their teacher was present throughout, but made the decision to listen for most of the time and then to fine-tune her short-term plans by bringing in a dog's skull and a skeleton over the next two weeks.

The REPEY/EPPE team describe this kind of relaxed exchange as 'sustained shared thinking' and emphasise, from their observations, that this crucial support for young learning, will not happen if the day is tipped towards a great deal of adult-initiated and adult-led activities or exchanges. Marion Dowling has explored this concept through visual examples, from across the age range of early childhood, and shows that, of course, adult-initiated experiences can support young learning. However, the time and space planning has to allow generous opportunities for hands-on experiences, children's own conversations and an adult role that involves coming alongside young thinking – not taking it over. The practical messages from different projects are consistent.

Early Years Foundation Stage strand

Designing and making

- Build and construct with a wide range of objects, selecting appropriate resources, and adapting their work where necessary
- Select the tools and techniques they need to shape, assemble and join materials they are using

Information and communication technology (ICT)
- Find out about and identify the uses of everyday technology and use information and communication technology and programmable toys to support their learning

---

Using tools and technology

Five-year-olds can be competent with a wide range of tools in art, craft, woodwork, construction and domestic skills such as food preparation and cooking. The potential for learning is real, so a great deal depends on the experiences available to children and how adults (parents as well as practitioners) have resolved the balance between safety concerns and enabling children to learn the skills. See, for instance, the examples in *What Does it Mean to be Four?* about children and the woodwork table (page 58), a resource that is most likely to raise adult anxiety levels.

The only reference to ICT in the Foundation Stage is within one single Early Learning Goal in this area of knowledge and understanding of the world. The EYFS has not changed this situation. Furthermore, the goal is not exclusively about computers. Young children need to become computer literate in a technological world, but there is no tearing hurry. Five-year-olds can be adept with different resources within information and communication technology, including use of computers. However, good practice needs to develop in this relatively recent area for children's learning and adult understanding.

- Five-year-olds can be interested in everyday technology in their own home, early years setting and the local neighbourhood. They can have grasped how to work some familiar technology such as television and video remote controls. Some five- and six-year-olds are adept at simple programming of domestic appliances.
- Five-year-olds, who have been enabled to have experience of technological equipment, can be careful as well as understanding how to use equipment, such as simple calculators, cameras, including sometimes a digital camera, video and audio tape recorders and programmable toys.
- Five-year-olds are often fascinated by local technology such as closed circuit television, automatic doors and bar scanners in the supermarket.
- In terms of computer literacy, five-year-olds can show that they understand the basic programs of which they have experience and can have grasped the main visual elements of computers as a resource.

Because computer technology is relatively new, early years, school and out-of-school teams can welcome advice about the most appropriate ways to use computers with young children. The DATEC project led by John Siraj-Blatchford and Iram Siraj-Blatchford, is a source of well considered advice. They also undertook the KidSmart project in collaboration with IBM and Early Education. The DATEC team suggests that children's learning within ICT has two equally important strands:

1. Development of an emergent technological literacy and children's understanding of the uses of ICT
2. Developing children's practical capability with the tools that are offered by ICT

As the team emphasise, the adults who aim to support children's learning in these two strands need to have that understanding and confidence themselves. Support and friendly training for the adults is often the crucial first step to helping children to learn most effectively.

The valuable advice from the DATEC project is also discussed in *What Does it Mean to be Four?* Some themes are revisited and extended here for the five-year-olds.

- Practitioners, and parents in partnership, need to ensure that ICT applications are genuinely educational and can support children's learning.
- A great deal of computer software is labelled and promoted as 'educational' - a powerful buzz word, but all software needs to be considered with an open mind.
- Some packages for language and number drill have narrow learning scope. The skills can be far better practised by children using real materials, than on the screen.
- Some programs follow a directive form of teaching style with simplistic rewards. Young children are much better served by finding their own satisfaction and through direct communication with appreciative adults.
- Another problem of some so-called 'educational software' is the closed problem-solving format. On screen this works as a series of options, only one of which is correct. Children learn to try each option in turn until they hit the 'right' button. Such a strategy does not support more challenging problem-solving and the active thinking of which five-year-olds can be capable. Children may not even have grasped why this option is the correct one. They just know it is correct, because that choice has released the sound or smiley reward.

Early years, school and out-of-school teams need to look for ICT use that enables children to work together. Young children need materials that encourage them to experience ICT, including computers, as a resource that can be used alongside other play, writing and mathematical resources. The sense of integration of ICT is supported when settings have the computer table central, not somewhere separate in a room off the main activity area. If children are to grow in understanding of ICT, they need to see it used in a meaningful context and for recognisable purposes. Otherwise, ICT, especially the computer, falls into a category of being used continuously for its own sake, until someone stops you.

ICT should be promoted as part of the resources available to children, as of potential interest but neither as a 'have to' option nor as something so special it is restricted to a treat. Practitioners need to avoid using time on the computer as a reward, or withdrawing it as a consequence of general disruptive behaviour.

Understanding time and place

Five-year-olds are often interested in their local environment, from the outdoor space of their early year settings to local open spaces and the neighbourhood as a whole. They make sense of the natural world from what they can see, touch, hear and smell locally and from that perspective can build a strong basis for the growth of their general knowledge.

For example

When I visited Windale First School in Oxford, some of the Reception class children were involved in gardening. This was a long-term project in which the children were absorbed. On this day, several children were busy digging in potatoes and onions in the bed outside. Others were potting seedlings in bought compost indoors. The children used small size but proper gardening tools and were accompanied by a parent helper.

The teacher used the review time at the end the morning to encourage the gardeners to talk about their activity to the other children. She also used the time in a friendly way to reinforce safe use of tools. The four- and five-year-olds were pleased to explain and show their peers how to carry a spade (pointed downwards) and to confirm, when asked by the teacher, 'do we run?', 'No, we walk'.

Windale is not the only Reception or nursery class that I have known to do gardening with the children. A real growing project helps children to understand far more than can be communicated with books. Other early years settings have also discovered that it is important to involve the children in the hands-on restructuring of their outdoor space. It can seem more efficient to do the digging and carrying over a weekend, with adult volunteers. But it is much better to organise the work so that the children can discuss what will be done, learn about the outdoors and be part of the physical work.

Since my visit to Windale, I have also encountered some nurseries and primary schools who have taken on their own allotment, as well as further examples of primary schools who have re-organised part of the school grounds for this purpose. This kind of long-term commitment has been met with enthusiasm by children and a willingness to put in hard physical work on their piece of land. As practitioners explain to me, it is possible to deliver aspects from across the whole early years and school curriculum through re-connecting children with how the natural world actually works. It is also a project that benefits from the involvement of adults from the local community and not only families of children who currently attend a setting.

Five-year-olds have a sense of time: of the present, the past and future to an extent but their perspective is personal and their time line is still not that of an adult. For many five-year-olds the most interesting events are local and within their own family and social group. By exploring their family and immediate neighbourhood, five-year-olds build the basis to history. But past and present has to have meaning for children now. In this area of learning, adults need to tune into what five-year-olds already know and how any new information or perspectives are, therefore, likely to connect for the children.

et, five- and six-year-olds can also be aware of major events - local, national and international. They watch television, see pictures in newspapers before they can read the text and will hear adults talking. Practitioners and parents need to acknowledge how significant national and international events, that reach the news, affect children as well as adults. Some of this information will be about exciting, special events. However, some will continue to be about distressing and frightening natural disasters, from around the globe, as well as destruction caused by human actions through terrorism. Additionally, it is inevitable that children are now aware of the saturation coverage, by news reports and endless speculation, following what are judged to be newsworthy tragedies involving children.

Four- and five-year-olds try to make sense of new experiences by connecting them to ideas they already understand. However, disturbing events may be hard to grasp and adult distress and confusion will make the task even harder for children.

- They need straight and honest answers to their questions and some of your answers can be factual. A question like 'do we have volcanoes in our country?' can be met with an honest 'no', with the interesting addition that many, many years ago we did and the remains are in places like Dartmoor.
- Four- and five-year-olds may ask some hard questions to which there is no simple answer. News images of starving children may bring the fair question of, 'why haven't the children got any food?' The answer may be that the harvest has failed and there are no shops, but war and fighting also disrupts the food supply.
- The murder or disappearance of children raises difficult issues that adults may prefer to avoid. But children need information that they can understand. They are learning about the world, its distressing aspects as well as happy. Adults need to be careful that five- and six-year-olds have an accurate framework in which to make sense of events. For this kind of event, children need parents and teachers to be honest, to explain with care that this kind of event does happen, but that it is very unusual and that is one reason why there was so much news coverage.

Early Years Foundation Stage strand - Communities
- Begin to know about their own cultures and beliefs and those of other people

Personal identity and culture

Five-year-olds are learning about all the indicators of group identity as well as their own personal development. It is important for practitioners to register carefully the 'begin to know' part of this Early Learning Goal. Knowing and understanding are at an early stage and it can be helpful for adults to think about how they learned about their own culture as well as how they learned about cultures that were unfamiliar to them. The heading on this strand of learning has been changed from 'Cultures and beliefs' to 'Communities'. I think this change of wording is a better reflection of young learning, right up to and including fives.

Cultural identity, one's own and recognition of the sources of identity for others, is a slow, steady process. Early years practitioners can make a difference through extending children's experiences and reflecting as adults on how best to introduce activities and follow through in conversation. However, it is crucial to be realistic in this area of learning and to acknowledge the power of learning from outside, as well as inside, any early years setting.

Food for thought

It is an important message to children how adults organise any celebration. You need to show equal respect to each event that you choose to celebrate. Part of that respect in practice is how much time you devote. What message do you give to children, and families, if one celebration continues for weeks and another is allocated a single day?

There is good reason for not stretching out any celebration or festival for ages, especially in terms of a rigid adult plan. If children are interested, then they will let you know that they want to do more cooking of this food or they would like this CD to become part of the permanent resources in their music corner.

No religious celebration, nor a more secular festival, exists in order to provide material for the early years or school curriculum. Some materials I have read get too close to this implication, and the approach leads to disrespect. There is also a risk that children's interest is disrupted if there is no choice other than making this card or other artefact, which is the next activity on the list.

- Five-year-olds can recognise difference and the aim of support in the early years is to build the outlook that different does not inevitably mean better or worse. Children can understand how feelings, family and childhood events can be a shared experience across social and cultural groups. There may be differences in how recognisable events are organised, like welcoming a new baby or local community celebrations.
- Five-year-olds can also recognise that people look different and that again different does not mean better or worse; it is just different. For some children those physical differences based on ethnic group will be obvious locally. For other children the awareness of difference will come through books, pictures and television images.
- A sensible approach by adults to children's understanding of cultural difference has to be grounded in the local community. Five-year-olds' experience to date is inevitably going to differ between children who live in an ethnically diverse area and those, of whom there are many in the UK, who live in a neighbourhood where there is little obvious ethnic diversity.
- There is little point in introducing any four- and five-year-olds to a long list of cultural and religious celebrations. They do not have the knowledge base to make sense of them. Without care, one celebration merges into another or is explained inappropriately by the culture or faith most familiar to children or adults.
- All five-year-olds need a sound basis of understanding of their own cultural identity and faith, if appropriate, before they are able to make sense of a less familiar basis for identity. Young children need to have connections of meaning and these will often be through the experiences of children who may initially look very different from themselves. It can be a challenge for adults to tune into what will make sense for fives. A nursery in Manchester developed a valuable resource in collaboration with children and families, which forms part of the *Festivals* series of DVDs. For more details see page 73.

Exploring celebrations can help to extend five-year-olds' understanding beyond their own back yard, but a great deal depends on how this experience is offered. Some early years teams feel that they have to organise a long list of celebrations, with the assumption that the experience will promote knowledge and positive attitudes. This result is only likely if you and your colleagues reflect on what you provide and how:

- Adults need to set a good example of showing respect and an effort to understand what will sometimes be unfamiliar customs.

- You need to make some choices; a long list helps nobody. A practical plan is to celebrate the key festivals of families whose children attend your setting. Then add, at most, one or two festivals over the year that will be new for everyone.
- You should take a distinctive approach to each celebration or festival. Definitely do not explain one celebration in terms of the beliefs or events of a religion more familiar to you.
- Look for opportunities to involve parents and the local community in any celebration and be ready to learn from them. You would usually respect parents' wishes if they feel strongly that they do wish their child to be involved in a given celebration. No celebration should last so long that a child who is withdrawn misses many other learning experiences.
- It is an important message to children how adults organise any celebrations. You need to show equal respect to all celebrations. Part of respect in practice is how much time you devote and whether it is unequal.

Negative outlooks

Young children become aware of the adult attitudes prevalent in their neighbourhood, initially from within their own family and then from an awareness of what is said and shown in the larger neighbourhood. Children are building their own attitudes and their awareness of differences will begin to be merged with a judgement about whether, and in what way, those differences matter. In neighbourhoods where there is tension between ethnic groups then five-year-olds can be well aware of this and express negative views about people from those defined other groups.

But, of course, tension is not exclusively based on cultural or ethnic differences. More than one generation of children has now been raised in Northern Ireland during what this community calls 'The Troubles'. Adults often prefer to believe that young children do not yet notice and cannot have been affected by the disruptions and deaths. However, young children are aware and begin to understand the importance of the different symbols that relate to Catholic and Protestant groups in the Province: flags, football teams, different leisure activities and symbolic annual events like marches.

Paul Connolly has shown that even some three-year-olds are aware of distinctions between the religious and social groups, but that by five years of age there is a high awareness of the impact of sectarianism. Apart from the age of the children and their likely increased understanding as a result of development, most four- and five-year-olds in Northern Ireland enter primary schools that have a clear religious affiliation. There are few integrated schools in the province.

The application of equal opportunities and anti-discriminatory practice in Northern Ireland has meant anti-sectarianism: an active attempt to challenge religious discrimination and bigotry and to build positive connections between the communities and their children. Paul Connolly's research identifies that, not surprisingly, without such active work, many five-year-olds have learned to value their own religious identity, Catholic or Protestant, over the alternative and begin to make negative, sectarian comments about the community to which they know they do not belong.

Physical Development

Physical movement and activity is important for five-year-olds. Their physical skills will have progressed significantly from the two-year-old skills base, so long as they have been given:

- Plenty of relaxed time to explore, practise and enjoy using their physical skills
- Patient adult step-by-step help to learn techniques as well as safe use of tools and equipment
- Experiences that support them in self-confidence about the process of learning to apply large and fine movements. Children need to have directly experienced the sense of 'getting better at...' otherwise some five-year-olds can already have decided that they are 'no good at...' large-scale physical activity or use of tools in some crafts.

Foundation Stage strands -
- **Movement and space**

  Move with confidence, imagination and in safety
- Move with control and co-ordination
- Travel around, under, over and through balancing and climbing equipment
- Show awareness of space, of themselves and others

Using equipment and materials

- Use a range of small and large equipment
- Handle tools, objects, construction and malleable materials safely and with increasing control

The importance of movement

Five-year-olds need to be able to move. For children, just like us as adults, physical activity is closely linked with mental alertness and emotional well-being. When children are required to sit still and be quiet for long periods of time (long to them), the enforced inactivity makes children intellectually stale, they are less able to learn.

Five-year-olds can manage periods of sitting down and concentrating (see page 12), but extending these too far is counter-productive. Young children are not learning just because they are sitting still. For some children, their bottom will remain on the seat or mat, but their brain has gone somewhere more interesting. Some five-year-olds will be physically unable to stop fidgeting and their struggles risk being seen exclusively as a behaviour problem.

For example

- Carolyn Webster Stratton has the lovely idea of the Wriggle Space. This is an area of the classroom, ideally marked off visually, where children, or anyone, can go and move about for a few minutes.

She suggested that adults can, if need be, hand out a limited number of Wriggle Space tickets each day and then children trade in the tickets when they need to have a good wriggle.

Nicola Call and Sally Featherstone describe the idea of 'brain breaks'. This handy phrase covers the need to allow fives, and older children, to have physically active interludes to refresh them after a period of focussed concentration, that needs children to remain fairly still.

Physical skills of five-year-olds

With practice and enough activity, children have nearly all the basic physical skills by six or seven years of age. So five-year-olds are still honing their skills within large movement and fine manipulative skills. Children within primary school still need plenty of practice to refine skills, practise co-ordination and balance. They are also still learning how to integrate skills they have mastered into more complex sequences. For instance, six- or seven-year-olds can run and they can dribble a football at slow speed. But only the more practised, and possibly talented footballers, will be able to move at speed and still manage to dribble the ball.

There is considerable variation between five-year-olds and some of the differences are likely to be explained by experience, since physical skill and confidence requires opportunity and practice.

- Five-year-olds can be confident in running, climbing, jumping and simple balancing. The confidence level of children varies and some will look and feel 'bolder' than others. Children will now also have taken on board gender expectations and some children may have decided that certain activities are for the other sex, not their own.
- They can adjust use of their skills to watch out for other people but not all the time. Many five-year-olds are adept at adjusting their speed, yet crashes are still possible. In a busy play area children may make the wrong prediction for how to turn or avoid another child.
- So long as they are not confined for space, five-year-olds use their physical skills in spontaneous games that they create. Sometimes they develop complex pretend play to which they return day after day, with negotiated roles and scripts.
- Five-year-olds are now ready to tackle the more complex movements involved in physical sequences such as skipping, hopping or hopscotch games or high speed catch. If you watch five-year-olds you will see that this application of their separate skills is not always easy at all.
- Some five-year-olds have gained the balance needed to manage equipment with a narrow base: two-wheeled bikes without stabilisers, roller or ice skates. Often the most difficult part of these skills for children to learn is to move from stationary to moving forward.
- Not all five-year-olds can manage these skills; especially if they have had limited opportunities. You will also notice that some five- and six-year-olds seem to have considerably less confidence than their peers. Some children never learn to ride a two-wheeled bike.
- Five-year-olds, who have benefited from plenty of relaxed practice, are mostly safe at judging what they can manage in physical skills in familiar and unpressurised surroundings.
- Problems can arise for even confident five-year-olds, if distraction means they lose their balance. They may also make a less safe judgement in unfamiliar surroundings, or if subjected to dares from other children.

- Five-year-olds are still lacking in the general knowledge that enables them to make sound judgements over road safety.
- Children usually have a confident sense of bodily awareness and are sensitive to the messages of their own body. They occasionally like to create a sense of imbalance deliberately by hanging upside down or spinning around to the point of total dizziness.

Five-year-olds can enjoy games organised, or facilitated, by adults. It is wise for adults to avoid a heavy emphasis on competition and winning or losing, for the sake of children's emotional development. But games can also be well, or poorly, run to suit five- and six-year-old physical skills:

- Children now show much more confident physical control and co-ordination of hands, feet and vision. They are more accurate throwers and kickers and can handle a wider range of games equipment.
- But, compared with older children and teenagers, the majority of five- and six-year-olds look 'clumsy' when they handle a bat or racquet or try to throw a ball with accuracy. This apparent lack of co-ordination with fine tuning the large physical movements is normal for this age range.
- Five-year-olds need adults who organise and join in games that are made enjoyable and non-competitive. You need to pitch or kick a ball to young children, so that it is easier for them to connect and return it. It is only with children well into middle childhood that you can reasonably play games in which you make it hard for them to connect.

For example

In Poplar Play the six summer playscheme children headed off for the park round the back of the centre with a practitioner and their equipment. The group included Yasmin and Sam (both seven years old) and Simone, Kimberley, Kayleigh and Damian (all five years old).

- The children were all keen to play the physical movement games guided by the practitioner. They did limbering up exercises with the adult: arm circling, head moving, waist movements. All the children could do the movements, the two seven-year-olds just looked a bit more co-ordinated and confident. Even within the same age, there were also individual differences. Simone and Kimberley were both five years old, Kimberley looked more flexible in her movements and physically co-ordinated.
- Everyone found it harder to balance on one leg and move the other one at the same time. There was much giggling and over-balancing. Then they did a jog round with two special moves, indicated when the practitioner called out a number: a knees bend, touch the ground and a jump in the air. Then everyone ran round the practitioner as she stayed still, then in the opposite direction. After the warm-up, the practitioner took the group through a range of games with racquets that made the co-ordination easier. This practitioner was also experienced with over-eights. She commented to me in conversation how much adults have to adjust games for the five- to seven-year-olds, if they are to enjoy the activity and not find it far too difficult.
- In pairs the children had one bean bag and a racquet each. They had to pass the bean bag between them. How many passes before it drops? They counted as they passed. There was a choice whether to tip the bean bag or toss it. Both actions required concentration and the children focussed well. Kayleigh showed an effective wrist action to flip the bean bag onto her partner's racquet. Tossing or tipping still took a co-ordination that was tricky for this age group, although much easier than trying to hit balls that bounce away from your racquet.
- Then the children stood spread at gaps around a marked circle and used the racquets like a low-held bat to move the ball between each other. They counted how many passes before

the ball went out of the circle and had to be fetched. It was difficult for children to hit the ball softly. When they hit too hard, it shot out of the circle. Even the seven-year-olds missed as well as the fives and there was much friendly comment from the children - 'you have to pay attention' and 'you were daydreaming'.

Then, still in the circle, the children had to bat the ball to each other around the edge of the circle. They were on bent knees and again they focussed well.

The children now said that they wanted to play tennis and some announced confidently that 'I can play tennis'. They tried in pairs and, although they seemed to have fun, it was a useful reminder that the physical actions were difficult. It was hard to connect with the ball, to drop the ball so they could hit it and connect back. The practitioner showed how hitting a ball against the wall was a bit easier.

For the last bit of time in the park, the group moved over to the play area. All the children were physically confident here. Even the five-year-olds had no problem negotiating a hanging clamber rope structure, even when it was swaying with their movements. They were all able to work the swing, if they had a push to start the movement. Even the youngest could do the co-ordination of legs, arms and whole body that was required to keep up the movement of the swing and increase the height. There were some differences, for instance Kayleigh had developed a more effective movement than Simone, but both were able to propel themselves.

Application of physical skills in self-care and play

In much the same ways as younger children, five-year-olds combine what we describe as the larger physical movements with fine co-ordination. They can also be skilled with the finer movements involved in close work and self-care. You will be able to observe the progress that has been made by five-year-olds. Their skills are shown by the fact that by this age they can often manage by feel. They can talk and dress at the same time, because they do not have to look all the time at what they are doing.

- Five-year-olds can be adept in using eyes, fingers and the relevant tools in woodwork, different kinds of construction, artwork, crafts and needlework. Five-year-olds who have been allowed and encouraged to take their time over projects can be highly motivated to continue with an activity that spans days.
- In project work children's physical skills work together with their ability to listen, look, talk about options in a project and planning ahead.
- Fine skills enable children to manage the physical co-ordination needed for forming letters or numbers in their writing. They need to move from a whole hand grasp to the finer fingers and thumb hold. Some children find this harder than others. Five-year-olds will be ready for this task and many will have fine-tuned the skills through relaxed activities involving large movements as much as the fine ones.
- Many five-year-olds will now show a clear preference for their right or left hand and about eight out of nine children are right-handed. More boys than girls are

left-handed and some children do not finalise their preference until seven or eight years of age. Some children, and adults, continue to use both hands in a flexible way for different tasks.

The importance of the playground

From five-year-olds' point of view, social and physical skills are not restricted to the boundaries of the Reception classroom. In Year 1 primary school life, playtime and experiences in the playground are important to children. Children need time and space to play in breaks and lunchtime in order to use their physical skills and recharge their emotional batteries before further class time.

The layout of school grounds varies between schools. Some five-year-olds may have their own area, perhaps shared with the nursery children. Some schools are able to have lower and upper primary playgrounds: an advantage when the ten- and eleven-year-olds look large to five-year-olds. Some five-year-olds and rising sixes have to manage the main playground and, in a poorly organised space, an integrated playground can be a scary place.

Some primary school teams have proper consultation with the children, but most discussion about school break times has been shaped by adult concerns. There can be limited acknowledgement of children's input on how they view the opportunities and any problems of the playground. Unreflective primary school teams tend to perceive break time mainly in terms of problems rather as offering potential for play. In 1994, Peter Blatchford and Sonia Sharp emphasised that children were the real experts on what went on in their playground and that any initiatives that aimed to improve playtime or school playgrounds would not get far unless adults listened to the views of children. Over a decade later, the research of Peter Blatchford and Sonia Sharp, and their insightful observations of the dynamics of the playground, are as relevant as ever.

The playground can be seen as a source of trouble, by adults or children, in terms of aggressive play or bullying. There can be risks for the youngest and smallest ones in a primary playground. So, there needs to be negotiation about space so that the livelier games can co-exist with other activities. Some of these playground issues are very real and concern is also felt by the children. But they do not appreciate, nor can they learn from sudden bans with no discussion.

Adults may claim that children stand about aimlessly or have no idea how to play. Children often welcome some playground equipment and playful, rather than nagging, adults. But observation of some primary school playgrounds suggests that adults are often busy banning games that children want to play, whilst complaining that 'children nowadays don't know how to play anymore'.

It is possible that many adults in school have always underestimated the importance of break times to children. The general lower status of playground support staff reflects the perspective that play time is less valuable. An increasing sense of pressure on primary school teams has led to cutbacks in children's play time based on the rationale that it is less valuable time, the priority is to get through the curriculum and that break times are optional. Peter Blatchford reported a national survey from the 1990s that more than a half of primary schools had reduced the children's breaks within the school day by decreasing the time given for lunch break and stopping any afternoon break. Anecdotal evidence suggests that the reduction has not necessarily halted. The associated problems of unrealistically short lunch breaks are that children either eat their food without having time to properly digest or do not eat enough. Their priority is to get out to play.

Many researchers, like Peter Blatchford, Sonia Sharp and also Wendy Titman have built a detailed picture of how children spend their time in primary school grounds during break times. Observation of what children actually do, and what they tell researchers they do in play, has shown the great variety around the country (see my books *Understanding children's play* and *Understanding children and young people* for further discussion of this area of practical research.) Break time and friendly and accessible school grounds are important to children because:

- Children engage in a wide range of physical activities: impromptu ball games, chasing and hiding, using the playground markings and equipment like hoops and skipping ropes when they are available.
- Pretend and fantasy games may last over days, as children return to the same theme from one break time to another.
- Seasonal games evolve such as using conkers, making daisy chains and kicking through leaves.
- Children enjoy conversation and just hanging out together with friends. They also like chatting with responsive playground support staff.
- Preparing for play can be just as important to children as the actual play. Children can be involved as they choose the activity for today, select who will be involved and their roles. An equally important part of play can be the search for an appropriate space or particular place in which to play a given game.
- Play is a time valued by children in primary school and they need this time to recharge their intellectual and emotional reserves. Children recognise some of the problems in poorly organised or equipped playgrounds. They appreciate effective adult help that includes proper consultation with children as users of school grounds.

Foundation Stage strand - Health and bodily awareness
- Recognise the importance of keeping healthy and those things which contribute to this
- Recognise the changes that happen in their bodies when they are active

Health knowledge and habits

There is a great deal of concern now that too many children are not physically active and that, combined with an unbalanced diet, this situation puts them at a high risk of obesity, with all the related risks to health. Observation of young children soon tells you that they do not want to sit still for long periods of time. Given sufficient time and space opportunities, fives are as happy as their younger selves, to be physically active – quite active enough for health reasons. Children across middle childhood may enjoy some lively PE in school and well-judged team games. But they do not need their physical activity to be organised all the time by adults; freely chosen, active play does the job very well.

So what is happening to prevent or slow down potentially active children? When practice is not child-friendly, the main culprits seem to be:

- An overloaded early years and school curriculum, which requires children to sit still for excessive stretches of indoors learning and which also dismisses the power of outdoor and active learning.
- Excessive worry about risks from ordinary play activities, such that children's outdoor space is boring and/or their time there is severely restricted.

- Adults who have forgotten how to play, or who are perplexed about how to be a playful companion to children, because they have emerged from a very sedentary childhood themselves.

It will be of very little use if practitioners focus their efforts on telling fives what they should do about healthy habits, if the daily experiences do not enable children to put that into continuous practice. In contrast, thoughtful reception and primary school teams have faced this challenge.

For example

Over recent years Crabtree Infant School has continued to develop their outdoor space and play resources – for children in Years 1 and 2, not only for the reception class. Like other teams who are committed to a nurturing environment in the school, they have also taken through, with their school cook, a serious overhaul of menus for lunchtime. I have listened to other, equally committed, practitioners (without the opportunity also to visit) and the consistent messages are that:

- Changes about food take time and are more effective when efforts are made to consult with children. Jamie Oliver's television programme about school dinners was essential to expose the scandal about food on the cheap for children. However, a significant change of this nature will not work within just a few months.
- When children have generous time for outdoor play, they are refreshed for indoor learning and the kind of concentration that is increasingly required for the school curriculum. Sensible school teams also view the school grounds as a direct extension of indoor facilities – the outdoor classroom.
- Children need to be kept safe from avoidable accidents, but trying to reduce perceived risk to zero is a hopeless task, and disrupts learning through play. Risk assessment and management is a matter of adult responsibility, but needs an approach in which the grown-ups think through all the consequences of their decisions. You can follow up these crucial issues in my *Too safe for their own good?* and Tim Gill's *No fear: growing up in a risk-averse society.*

These goals within the area of physical development remind us of the crucial role of the adult in listening, looking, talking with children about what interests them and setting a good example. The evidence is of the power of social learning and not of inevitable developmental stages. Children learn in this area of their development by steady practice, simple explanations, encouragement and appreciation from adults. In a friendly atmosphere, five-year-olds usually want to follow adults' example.

- Five-year-olds can have developed healthy habits such as hand-washing and cleaning their teeth, washing up crockery or putting their clothes for washing at home. But such habits do not develop solely because of their age. Children develop healthy, or unhealthy, habits because of the direction provided by adults within their family and the pattern in an early years or school setting.
- Children may have some idea of taking care against the weather - either cold and wet or hot. But they still need friendly adult reminders and guidance about putting on coats and taking effective care against the sun.
- Five-year-olds can have developed habits of healthy eating and drinking. Children learn from what key adults in their life have told them and shown them by example. Difficulties can arise when children have taken on distorted adult concerns about

health, such as 'being too fat' or the misleading approach of 'bad and good foods'. Adults still have major responsibilities in this area to enable and encourage children to follow wise guidance.

- Five-year-olds can have extended their understanding about bodies. They tend to grasp how bodies work from their own experience and asking questions that they want to know. They still have many gaps in their knowledge about feeling well, feeling ill and which parts of their body hurt.

- With adult support, five-year-olds can have started to learn some sensible guidelines about what to do in everyday accidents, such as cleaning cuts.

Creative Development

Food for thought

Some early years practitioners lack confidence in their own creative abilities and are only too swift to say they 'can't paint' or that their singing 'sounds awful'. Such uneasiness does not help adults to support children's creative development. It may also underpin the adult worries that any final wall display should reflect well on them – rather than be an accurate reflection of children's own art and craft work.

Working with young children is such a fine opportunity, because they will not criticise you. They are convinced that you can sing, dance and draw – as well as being able to play a good game of football or simple cricket.

Early years practitioners do not have to be 'good at art'. Your skills are to make available a range of interesting materials and be a supporting presence as children get involved. You do not have to be trained in singing or be able to play an instrument, in order to promote the musical sides to creativity. Obvious enjoyment is definitely enough as you behave as a keen partner in music making with sound makers and join in impromptu as well as adult-initiated dance sessions.

Five-year-olds have many skills that can support their explorations and productions in a wide range of creative endeavours. They have skills of observation, of listening and looking that can support their learning of techniques and possibilities. Five-year-olds have the communication skills of words and body language and the ability to adjust their use of spoken language to express mood, message and to bring imagination to life. Five-year-olds vary a great deal and some are more reticent by nature, perhaps preferring the quieter, less public forms of creative expression.

The importance of skills and attitudes

As well as the impact of individual temperament, children's creativity will have been shaped by their experience. By five years of age children will have developed attitudes about creative activities on the basis of their experience, including adult behaviour. Their learning encompasses physical skills, thinking and communication skills and broad attitudes about the task and their own likely ability.

- Some five-year-olds show enthusiasm for a creative project, considering what they may do and how, trying out different methods and drawing on past learning for what works, how this technique might be used, and so on.
- Other five-year-olds have accepted the belief that so-called creative activities, at least within a group setting, mean doing what the adult tells you, copying this model, making a painting 'like this one'.
- This mechanical outlook develops when adults have behaved as if an activity must be creative because art and craft materials are on the table. Yet adult behaviour has been directive: what could be called the 'identical egg-box daffodils problem'. Five-year-olds learn the pattern: do adults want you to use your own initiative or should you follow the template?
- The experiences of five-year-olds also build their attitudes about the role of ability and their own ability. Do you draw and paint because it is enjoyable and everyone can find ways to use art materials? Or have five-year-olds accepted that their drawings or ways of using paint are never quite right and their productions are rarely 'good enough'?
- Five-year-olds are also sensitive to time and creative activities. Children have the memory and thinking skills to take time over a project, returning to it and reworking to their own satisfaction and a broad brief.
- Yet some have learned that time is limited, again perhaps in a group setting. Their experience tells them that you have to finish an art or craft project within the time limit set by the adults. The objective is the time boundary rather than satisfaction in a job well done.

In contrast, I have seen lively creative work when teams have shifted to a permanent resource – by table or trolley – where children have generous supplies of stationery and art materials, plus

Early Years Foundation Stage strand - Exploring media and materials

- Explore colour, texture, space, form and shape in two and three dimensions

wide range of tools. Children organise their own activities and learn that such materials are available to illustrate or document their own child-initiated projects.

For example

I listened to one early years team who had seen a significant change in children's behaviour when the adults moved away from a timed, adult-led activity when every child had to come and make a Christmas card. The team instead made available a well-resourced table that they called 'the Christmas card workshop' and left this provision for children (threes to fives) to access when and how they chose. They tracked the use of the workshop over the week and observed that every child made use of this resource, often more than once. The cards made, out of choice by every child, were varied and genuinely creative in style and use of materials.

Do look also at the valuable resource from Curiosity and Imagination, available on the Sure Start website (see page 71). This set of twelve open-ended projects is a good reminder of how genuinely creative enterprises can start with a child's idea, an adult-initiated experience and a continuing combination of the two.

Using materials

Five-year-olds are able to use their physical and thinking skills to explore a wide range of materials and use of techniques. They can apply their interests to skills in art, craft, construction and activities like cooking that are both creative and practical. Five-year-olds who are given relaxed exploration time are interested to use their senses as well as work towards making something in particular.

For example

At Poplar Play Centre Charlotte (three years old) and Kayleigh (five years old) were both at the table with flat trays filled with a pink, thick mixture. They both understood about putting on the overalls. Kayleigh was able to do it herself, but Charlotte asked me for help, especially with the Velcro fixing at the back.

I asked what the material was, and Kimberley (five years) who was nearby explained, 'it's cornflour.' Charlotte and Kayleigh were both concentrating on the material. Charlotte liked to feel and smooth it with her fingers. Some of the mixture got onto her finger tips and she worked it off with care. She used the spoon to scrape and watched it dribble thickly back on the tray. Kimberly used the spoon as a tool to scrape and carve patterns, then smooth it out. She announced in a friendly way to Charlotte, 'me and Simone played with this this morning. Not you.'

Five-year-olds can have an impressive repertoire of songs, rhymes and associated hand movements. Their general musical ability and positive attitudes towards music making can lead to some impressive

Early Years Foundation Stage strand - Creating music and dance
- Recognise and explore how sounds can be changed, sing simple songs from memory, recognise repeated sounds and sound patterns and match movements to music

self-organised music sessions (see the example). Ideally, singing is an enjoyable activity for children and happy four and five-year-olds show spontaneous outbreaks of song. Children can enjoy adult-led singing and music making, when such sessions support everyone's talent and boost the sense of enjoyment in such an activity. But it is preferable that adults also break into song and join in with children in an informal way during the day.

Five-year-olds are not just little versions of adults; they have smaller lungs and they tend to breathe in and out more frequently. So it is not helpful to tell them to sing up more loudly; this request just results in children who strain to sing and verge on shouting, not singing. You will help by encouraging children to sit up, if they are in a seated position, and to think about taking big breaths.

For example

On the trip to the park from Poplar Play Centre in the morning, the children had each carried a plastic racquet. Before we had left the centre they were playing them as guitars and then in

e park some of them had positioned the racquets like violins, under their chin and they were
roducing a completely different kind of music. The violin singing was high pitched and with
lenty of la-las. On the way back from the park, the impromptu pretend music session started
pontaneously once more. This time the racquets became a whole series of instruments, as the
roup of six children worked their way through the song, 'I can play the piano, piano, piano …
nd saxa-saxa-saxaphone'.

fter lunch, the playscheme group had returned to energetic singing of the piano song. The
ractitioner suggested in a friendly way, 'Why don't we make the home corner the singing room
or a while, so you don't disturb other people.' The suggestion was met with enthusiasm and most
f the group headed off. Yasmin and Kimberley stayed to make a piano with sheets of paper. They
hose red and grey to make alternate coloured keys.

ll the playscheme children (five- and seven-year-olds) accompanied by Michael (two years) set
hemselves up in the home corner and ran a long singing and then dance session of their own
ccord. The group did many rounds of the piano song. They followed with a well orchestrated
ersion of 'hey, hey baby - I wanna know-o-o, if you'll be my girl'. They were able to hold a firm
eat, close harmony and well timed oohs and aahs that fitted the words. They were now equipped
ith instruments - most children had pairs of sticks, but also a tambourine. They held closely to
me, followed the rhythm and were able to dance as well as sing simultaneously.

maginative flair and ideas

ive-year-olds can have a rich imagination that they apply in creative activities and through
heir play. The shift in balance of activities within a Reception class and Year 1 may mean that
xpression through pretend play becomes steadily more possible only during break times in the
chool grounds. The layout and timetable of some, not all, Reception classes may mean that role
lay and other applications of imagination within children's play have less scope within the more
ormal parts of the school day. (See page 58 about play in school and school grounds.)

Being a helpful adult

Adult input via open-ended questions can be valuable, but watch out that you do not overdo the commentary or the
questions.

Bernadette Duffy shares a valuable story in her book on creativity (on page 100). She tells how five year old Shayma
brought a drawing but held it behind her back and would not show it until Bernadette promised not to ask, 'do tell me
about it'. Shayma explained that sometimes she just wanted to show something and not talk about it at all; that some
things were just for looking at.
All adults could learn from this cautionary tale: about reflecting on our own words and actions, but also that five-year-
olds who trust us will give valuable feedback on our own adult behaviour, we just have to listen.

Early Years Foundation Stage strand -

Responding to experiences, expressing and communicating ideas

- Respond in a variety of ways to what they see, hear, smell, touch and feel

- Express and communicate their ideas, thoughts, feelings by using a widening range of materials, suitable tools, imaginative and role play, movement, designing and making, and a variety of songs and musical instruments

For example

Creativity can unfold in many different ways and with equipment that initially looks unlikely. I enjoyed a presentation from Alan Paterson of the University of Aberdeen on his explorations of light with young children. Amongst other items, Alan Paterson uses an overhead projector with four- and five-year-olds. Children are fascinated by it and soon learn to explore the possibilities. Some of the ideas include:

- Items look different when placed on the surface and projected onto the screen: a large green plant bowl, cake tins, little objects alone or in a pattern.
- Children relish the shadow play that is possible with hands or puppets.
- They are able to place themselves against the screen with an image projected onto their own body.
- Some projectors are flexible enough to enable you to direct an image on to the floor and children can 'get into' the image and play.
- Children can make and project their own drawings on acetate.

Part of children's developing creativity is a sense of aesthetic appreciation. Five-year-olds, who are confident their opinions are valued, will start to express views and preferences in art, music, dance. They will have likes and dislikes in art forms and music and experiences in nursery and Reception can extend the children's horizons to forms of creative expression that are less familiar to them.

Undoubtedly some five-year-olds will show particular flair in some areas. A balanced approach by adults can encourage those five-year-olds whose talents develop within particular forms of creative expression. Yet it is possible to support five-year-olds towards attitudes of enjoyment in creative activities, building a basis for satisfying leisure activities and hobbies.

Five-year-olds can think ahead and consider materials and possible ways to create something, as well as ways to overcome problems. Given time and encouragement they are able to weigh up possibilities, make some choices and compare results. They recall past experiences so can often use their memory of how to create a particular effect, including suitable techniques and tools. Supportive adults can have helped this learning, and continue to support, by friendly demonstration, sharing good techniques and appropriate short cuts and enabling children to get enough practice.

For example

Out-of-school care (after-school clubs and holiday playschemes) often enable more mixing between the ages. One summer at Cool Kids at St. Joseph's in Cleethorpes, the older children

anned a talent contest. They organised much of the event themselves, liaising with adults as
cessary. They encouraged other children, including the youngest ones, without pressure to join
the range of different kinds of performances. The older children (only late primary school
e) arranged rehearsals and put on the final show.

he opportunities of out-of-school settings can also be that there is time, so an activity project
n last as long as it takes. In Cool Kids at St Josephs one summer project on recycling lasted the
tire summer playscheme. Children of all ages were closely absorbed in making a large item out
recycled materials and some impressive products resulted.

What should concern you?

Of course, five-year-olds are as varied a group as their two-, three- and four-year-old selves. The differences in individual temperament that you will have noticed in previous years will still be observable. Tendencies may be modified somewhat. Perhaps the more wary children have experienced that a bit of risk-taking can be safe and the more outgoing children have learned to moderate their liveliness depending on the situation. The behaviour and approach of some children may be a source of concern, perhaps continuing from when you knew them as younger children. You would be concerned about:

- Five-year-olds who seem uncertain about their own competence and ability to learn. Children can have decided by now that adults require high standards that they as children are unlikely to meet. It is serious if five and six years have concluded that they are 'stupid' or 'useless' at specific skills. Some five-year-olds can already show the signs that they are negative about school and this kind of learning experience.

- Some five- and six-year-olds will still struggle with their social skills. But you should notice children who do not have friends and appear to be disconnected from ordinary social interaction and play. They may have developmental disabilities within the autistic spectrum disorder and such a disability will not necessarily have been picked up so far.

- Non-specific language difficulties may not have fully emerged, especially if a child manages fairly well socially. As for the four-year-olds, there may be a number of reasons for children's difficulties. In partnership with parents there will be a need to check for undiagnosed hearing problems, very limited language experience to date, learning disabilities and language disorders.

- Five-year-olds can be bilingual already and some will be in the process of learning their second language. Children need plenty of appropriate support. If you do not speak a child's first language, it will not be obvious to you when he or she already has problems in the home language. You would need to ensure, in partnership with parents, that children get help swiftly if they are delayed in their first language or have problems of fluency, such as stammering.

- Five- and six-year-olds, who have experienced developmentally appropriate early literacy activities, can have sound building blocks to learning to read and write. I have been honest (pages 31) in my view, shared by others, that some of the Early Learning Goals in literacy are unrealistic. But it would be right to be concerned about a five-year-old, who had had proper early literacy experience yet did not seem to have understood the general ideas of print and the written language. Five years of age would be early to diagnose dyslexia, but it is sensible to track a child's struggles and what support can or cannot do to help.

- Five-year-olds still do not have perfect balance and some co-ordinations are still challenging for them (see page 55). But you would be right to be concerned if children had persistent difficulties with self-care skills, perhaps are always the last to manage to dress or complete daily routines. Children may also show their struggles

in emergent writing or artwork. There is the possibility of dyspraxia, when five- or six-year-olds look considerably less co-ordinated than their peers in physical skills or bodily awareness.

- You need to be concerned and talk with parents about any difficulties that raise issues about children's confidence in their physical skills or their ability to engage in close observation. Hearing and vision may be of concern. Partial or variable problems in hearing or sight have not always been identified by four or five years of age.
- Five-year-olds are still developing their understanding of some abstract ideas but they have mainly grasped the many ways to describe the world around them. Continuing confusion about basic ideas might mean a child needs extra help in paying close attention, for instance using the senses to experience 'same' and 'different' along the various dimensions. Continued confusion in distinguishing colours, after appropriate help, could mean that a child has some degree of colour blindness.
- Children take on the attitudes of their family and the local neighbourhood. Sometimes those attitudes will be negative. Practitioners in school and out-of-school care will need to address rejecting words and behaviour directly. Otherwise the rejection and offensiveness will only get stronger.

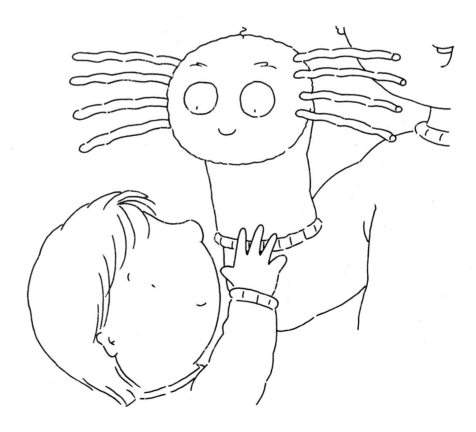

Further Resources

Accessing materials about the Early Years Foundation Stage (EYFS)

The EYFS applies to England, will be statutory (under the Childcare Act 2006) and must be fully implemented from September 2008.

- At that point the EYFS will replace both Birth to Three Matters (currently for under threes) and the Foundation Stage (currently three- to five-year-olds) to create a birth to five years early childhood framework that, as was the case with the Foundation Stage, definitely includes children in reception class.
- From September 2008 the Welfare Requirements will replace the set of separate booklets of the National Care Standards. Inspection will be under sections 49 and 50 of the Childcare Act 2006.

The EYFS materials are mainly provided within a pack entitled The *Early Years Foundation Stage – Setting the Standards for Learning, Development and Care for children from birth to five*. This pack includes:

- Two booklets: the Statutory Framework and the Practice Guidance.
- The single set of Welfare Requirements are in the Statutory booklet.
- The Practice booklet includes the birth to five years descriptive developmental material and suggestions for good practice.
- A poster about the EYFS – led through the four broad, guiding themes of A Unique Child, Positive Relationships, Enabling Environments and Learning and Development.
- A set of twenty-four Principles into Practice cards, which provide key ideas and examples about good practice. The Statutory booklet makes it clear that these materials are central for guiding good practice.
- A CD Rom, which includes all the main materials. This resource also provides briefing papers, website links and a series of brief video excerpts.

All EYFS materials can be ordered from DCSF Publications tel: 0845 60 222 60 -reference number 00012-2007PCK-EN. Materials are also on: www.teachernet.gov.uk/teachingandlearning/EYFS www.standards.dfes.gov.uk/EYFS

The EYFS Briefing Pack for local authorities includes materials to guide training about the birth to five framework. Much of this resource is also useful to group leaders/managers and to childminders. The reference number is 00106-2007BKT-EN. These materials are also on the Teachernet website – look down the left-hand side on the EYFS home page.

Revised editions of the EYFS booklets were published in May 2008, and placed on the Teachernet website. This site has a list of the changes and a Q&A section.

Books and websites

- Blatchford, Peter and Sharp, Sonia *Breaktime and the School: Understanding and Changing Playground Behaviour* (Routledge 1994)
- Bromley, Helen *Making My Own Mark: Play and Writing* (Early Education, 2006)
- Boxall, Marjorie *Nurture Groups in School: Principles and Practice* (Paul Chapman Publishing 2002)
- Brooker, Liz *Starting School: Young Children Learning Cultures* (Open University Press 2002)
- Caddell, Dorothy *Numeracy in the Early Years: What the Research Tells Us* (Scottish Consultative Council on the Curriculum 1998, can be downloaded from www. ltscotland.org.uk/earlyyears/images/numeracyinearlyyears_tcm4-124469.pdf)
- Call, Nicola and Featherstone, Sally *The thinking Child Resource Book* (Network Educational Press, 2003)
- Campbell, Robin *Literacy from Home to School: Reading with Alice* (Trentham Books 1999)
- Connolly, Paul; Smith, Alan and Kelly, Berni *Too Young to Notice: The Cultural and Political Awareness of 3-6 Year Olds in Northern Ireland* (Community Relations Council, 2002 tel: 028 9022 7555)
- Cremin, Hilary *Circle Time: Why it Doesn't Always Work* Primary Practice, The Journal of the National Primary Trust, Spring 2002, 30, 23-29
- Curiosity and Imagination (a project based at 4Children) *Inspiring Creativity and Imagination* 2005 - projects with children in early years centres download www. surestart.gov.uk/communications/childcareworkers/inspiringcreativity
- Department of Education Northern Ireland – information about developments on www.deni.gov.uk
  Donaldson, Margaret *Children's Minds* (Fontana 1978 – for discussion in a more recently published book see Lindon, 2005, below)
- Dowling, Marion *Supporting Young Children's Sustained Shared Thinking: An Exploration* (DVD and booklet, Early Education 2005, tel: 020 7539 5400 www.early-education. org.uk)
- Duffy, Bernadette *Supporting Creativity and Imagination in the Early Years* (Open University Press 1998)
- EPPE: The Effective Provision of Pre-School Education project - a wide range of papers on www.ioe.ac.uk/schools/ecpe/eppe
- Fabian, Hilary *Children Starting School: A Guide to Successful Transitions and Transfers for Teachers and Assistants* (David Fulton Publishers 2002)
- Fajerman, Lina; Jarrett, Michael and Sutton, Faye *Children as Partners in Planning: A Training Resource to Support Consultation with Children* (Save the Children 2000)
- Featherstone, Sally (ed) *L is for Sheep: Getting Ready for Phonics* (Featherstone Education 2006 www.featherstone.com.uk)
- Gill, Tim *No Fear: Growing Up in a Risk Averse Society* (Calouste Gulbenkian Foundation 2007 – summary and text of the book available on www.gulbenkian.org. uk)
- Ginsborg, Jane and Locke, Ann *Catching Up ... or Falling Behind?* 2002 www. literacytrust.org.uk/Pubs/ginsborg.html
- Hughes, Anne and Ellis, Sue *Writing it Right? Children Writing 3-8* (Scottish Consultative Council on the Curriculum 1998, can be downloaded from www. ltscotland.org.uk/earlyyears/Images/writingitright_tcm4-124463.pdf)
- Learning and Teaching Scotland has an early years section on www.ltscotland.org. uk/earlyyears/ and publications that can be downloaded listed on www.ltscotland. org.uk/search/index.asp

Learning Through Landscapes - an organisation focussed on developing the potential of school grounds and outdoor learning, www.ltl.org.uk

- Lewisham Early Years Advice and Resource Network *A Place to Learn: Developing a Stimulating Environment* (LEARN 2002 Tel: 020 8695 9806)
- Lindon, Jennie *Understanding Children's Play* (Nelson Thornes 2001)
- Lindon, Jennie *Too Safe for Their Own Good? Helping Children Learn about Risk and Life Skills* (National Children's Bureau 2003)
- Lindon, Jennie *Understanding Child Development: Linking Theory and Practice* (Hodder Arnold 2005)
- Lindon, Jennie *Equality in Early Childhood: Linking Theory and Practice* (Hodder Arnold 2006)
- Lindon, Jennie *Understanding Children and Young People: Development From 5-18 Years* (Hodder Arnold 2007)
- Lindon, Jennie *Safeguarding Children and Young People: Child Protection 0-18 years* (Hodder Arnold 2008)
- Marsden, Liz and Woodbridge, Jenny *Looking Closely at Learning and Teaching... A Journey of Development* (Early Excellence 2005)
- McGuinness, Carol *From Thinking Skills to Thinking Classrooms* 1999 DfEE Research Brief RB115 in Publications section of www.teachernet.gov.uk
  Moyles, Hargreaves et al *Interactive Teaching in the Primary Classroom: Digging Deeper into Meanings* (Open University Press 2003)
- Munn, Penny "What do children know about reading before they go to school?" 'in Owen, Pamela and Pumfrey, Peter (eds) *Emergent and Developing Reading: Messages for Teachers* (Falmer Press 1997)
- Munn, Penny '"Children's beliefs about counting" 'in Thompson, Ian (ed) *Teaching and Learning Early Numbers* (Open University Press, 1997) See also the discussion about Penny Munn's ideas in Ian Sugarman Reasons for counting (Primary Mathematics, Summer 2006, available on www.numbergym.co.uk/Docs/Reasons%20for%20counting.pdf)
- Palmer, Sue and Bayley, Ros *Foundations of Literacy: A Balanced Approach to Language, Listening and Literacy Skills in the Early Years* (Network Educational Press 2004)
- REPEY project *Researching Effective Pedagogy in Early Years*: Brief No 356: www.dfes.gov.uk/research/data/uploadfiles/RB356.doc
- Rich, Diane; Casanova, Denise; Dixon, Annabelle; Drummond, Mary Jane; Durrant, Andrea and Myers, Cathy *First Hand Experiences: What Matters to Children* (2005 tel: 01473 737405 www.richlearningopportunities.co.uk)
- Roberts, Joy *The Rhetoric Must Match the Practice* (Early Years Educator, volume 2 [5], 2000).
- Rose, Jim *Independent Review of the Teaching of Early Reading* DFES 2006 www.teachernet.gov.uk/publications
- Siraj-Blatchford, Iram and Siraj-Blatchford, John *More Than Computers:Information and Communication Technology in the Early Years* a report of the DATEC project and other practical advice (Early Education, 2003)
- Stacey, Hilary and Robinson, Pat *Let's Mediate* (Lucky Duck Publishing/Sage 1997)
- Stratton, Carolyn Webster *How to Promote Children's Social and Emotional Competence* (Paul Chapman Publishing 1999)
- Titman, Wendy *Special Places; Special People: The Hidden Curriculum of School Grounds* (Learning Through Landscapes/WWF UK 1994)
- Welsh Assembly - for information about the Foundation Phase in Wales http://new.wales.gov.uk/topics/educationandskills/policy_strategy_and_planning/earlywales/foundation_phase/foundation_phase_documents/?lang=en

- Whitebread, David et al *Developing Independent Learning in the Early Years A Report of the Cambridgeshire Independent Learning in the Foundation Stage Project* 2005 www.educ.cam. ac.uk/cindle/index.html

ideos/DVDs

heck the relevant organisation for current prices. The only free resources are from Sure Start, epartment of Children Schools and Families and Community Playthings.

Child's Eye MediaLtd - two DVDs of *A Childs Eye View of Festivals* tel: 0161 374 5509 www. childseyemedia.com•

Community Playthings *The Value of Unit Block Play* one of many videos/DVDs from this source tel: 0800 387 457 www.CommunityPlaythings.co.uk

- National Children's Bureau *Tuning Into Children* (Book and video tel: 020 7843 6000)
- Sightlines Initiative Rising Sun *Woodland Pre-school Project* (Visual and written materials tel: 0191 261 7666 www.sightlines-initiative.com)
- Siren Film and Video Ltd *Exploratory play* and other learning and play titles, tel: 0191 232 7900 www.sirenfilms.co.uk
- Sheffield University *REAL Project Early Literacy Education with Parents: a Framework for Practice* (Tel: 0114 222 0400)
- Sure Start – *Foundation Stage Toolkit* set of DVDs includes *Celebrating young children.* (Reference number DfES 1198-2005 GCDI, from the DCSF publications centre tel: 0845 6022 260.)

I have learned a great deal through discussions with early years practitioners and consultants and through visits to a wide range of early years settings. In connection with this book, I would especially like to thank the staff team and children at:

- Balham Family Centre and Latchkey Project, South London
- Bucks Kids' Club, Leek
- Cool Kids at St Josephs, Cleethorpes
- Crabtree Infants' School, Harpenden
- KidsComeFirst, Colchester
- Poplar Play Centre (referred to in brief as Poplar Play), East London
  Sun Hill Infant School, New Arlesford
  Thongsley Fields Primary and Nursery School, Huntingdon•
  Windale First School, Oxford
- Welholme Infants School, Grimsby

I would like to thank the following individuals whose ideas have been so valuable to focus on five-year-olds as children. The details given in brackets are the professional role of the individual at the time they provided the help.

- Cherry Baker (Deputy Head of Windham Nursery)
- Ros Bayley (Early Years Consultant)
- Annie Davy (Oxford EYDCP)
- Margaret Edgington (Early Years Consultant)
- Sue Martin (Head of Welholme Infants School)
- Penny Munn (Research Co-ordinator, Department of Childhood and Primary Studies, University of Strathclyde)
  Rachel Myer (Head of Thongsley Fields Primary and Nursery School)
- Iram Siraj-Blatchford (Professor of Early Childhood Education, Institute of Education)
- Penny Tassoni (Early Years Consultant)
- Wendy Titman (Specialist on the outdoors)
  Rosie Waring Green and Kim Owen Jones (Deputy Head and Head of Sun Hill Infant School)